"Yours Sincerely"

a biography of
Jack Williams

[handwritten inscription]

by

Frank Asbury

H. T. PRESS

Cover design by The Book Studio
Photo Credits:
Photos on covers and pages 23, 24, 29, 32, 34, 37, 40, and 87 courtesy KOY
Radio.
Photos on pages 64, 68, 77, 78, 79, 84 and 90 courtesy Arizona Historical
Society.
Photos on pages 3, 4, 48 and 66 courtesy Jack Williams.

Library of Congress Cataloging-in-Publication Data

Asbury, Frank
Yours Sincerely: a biography of Jack Williams / by Frank Asbury
    p.   cm.
Includes bibliographical references and index.
1. Williams, Jack, 1909-   2. Governors—Arizona—Biography.
3. Mayors—Arizona—Phoenix—Biography.   4. Arizona—Politics
and government—1951-   I. Title.
F815.3.W55A83   1994   94-5107
979. 1'053—dc20   CIP

ISBN #0-9640302-0-9

Printed in the United States of America

H T Press
12629 N Tatum Blvd #817
Phoenix AZ 85032

Contents

Thanks from Frank

I first met Jack Williams in 1964. He had already been working at KOY for 35 years. He had already been mayor of his city and mine. I wanted a job. He told me before I could become the radio man I so desired to be, I would have to learn to type. I went away. The radio job would have to wait.

I returned three months later, touch typing skills freshly learned. Jack hired me. Like dozens of other people who worked for Jack, I learned first-hand the man's word was gold. He could be trusted.

Today Jack Williams remains the same honest, straightforward, truly decent man his life has always defined.

Thanks, Jack, for permitting me to tell your story.

I'm grateful for your generosity in sharing personal family recollections, written material related to your professional and public service careers, your radio scripts and personal photographs. Without such input this book would not have been possible.

I am equally touched by the warmth, graciousness and hospitality shown my wife and me, by Vera Williams as we intruded, many times, into your busy life to do this work.

Thanks to Bill Lester, so much a part of radio's rise in the desert, for your help in painting the picture.

Thanks to Gary Edens for creating an atmosphere of challenge, growth, and opportunity for me during my tenure at KOY. Thanks for your perspective on Governor Jack, and for allowing me to raid the station's photo archives.

To my wife, Sally, my heartfelt appreciation and love. Your assistance in research, the hours spent scanning microfiche, your gentle but firm arguments on context and form along the way were most important. My great blessing, is your partnership in my life.

Frank Asbury

Foreword

My life has spanned most of the twentieth century! It has been the best of centuries and the worst.

At its beginning, life was simple and largely rural. Doors were left unlocked at night and people slept unharmed outside when the weather was warm. At its end, life was cheap and senseless killings, unrestrained use of guns, and anarchy on our streets.

Two World Wars marred my century, but religion and "our way of life" flourished! Charles Lindbergh, the "Lone Eagle" flew across the Atlantic into instant fame, only to have his child snatched away and killed. At the beginning, kidnapping of the child was headline news! At the end, only horrible mass massacres attracted headlines.

Electricity and its children brightened our lives, while radio —in which I found a lifetime career—made "a whispering gallery of the skies." Then television, with its magic box of colors, came into our homes.

My life paralleled the early *"Rags to Riches"* saga made prominent by Horatio Alger tales. The credo of work hard, be honest, don't try to take all the credit framed a man's mission.

Sometime mid-century our "children" revolted against the "system", authority, and their parents! "Hippies" and "Flower Children" took to the streets. Chicago had its "Days of Rage" when civilized behavior vanished.

That was the time of our Nation's "Loss of Innocence" and "Death of Conscience" in the young. This loss of responsibility for one's own actions has led us down a perilous path of senseless violence.

We cannot choose the century in which we are born. But, if I could, I would have selected the twentieth! We cannot select the century we die in; but I have a feeling that the latter part of the twentieth century has provided more violent ways to die than any in history—from the Atomic bomb to the careless use of cars and weapons.

Yet, I would not have chosen any other!

For me, personally—blessed by a wonderful wife for over fifty years, admirable children, warm supporters and friends—I have no quarrels and few regrets about my century!

Jack Williams

One-eyed Jacks Aren't Always Wild!

"No man undertakes a trade he has not learned, even the meanest. Yet everyone thinks himself sufficiently qualified for the hardest of all trades, that of government." — Socrates

In 1988, Arizona political history was made when its governor, Evan Mecham, was impeached. More history was made when Rose Mofford was sworn in to fill his unexpired term, thus becoming the state's first woman governor.

Members of the legislature were peevish following the impeachment. Because of a state budget dripping with red ink, and several other matters, legislative sessions became labored, marathon-like tests of endurance spiced with plenty of acrimony between members.

Three years after the Mecham impeachment, the legislature was tainted when some of its members were implicated in a vote buying sting operation labeled AZSCAM!

There was more.

The national savings and loan disaster was defined to a high degree by the failure of a California thrift headed by Charles Keating—of Phoenix, Arizona.

Arizona even took a hit in the world of sports. The National Football League, wielding the enormous economic club of its annual Super Bowl football game, pulled the 1993 game from Phoenix (Tempe, actually) after voters rejected a paid holiday honoring Dr. Martin Luther King Jr. (League owners later acknowledged an Arizona vote establishing the holiday and awarded the 1996 Super Bowl to Phoenix.)

Arizonans were repeatedly embarrassed by the perceptions

of their state from beyond her borders.

It wasn't always this way.

One-eyed Jack's Aren't Always Wild!

The tall, distinguished looking man, hair reflecting touches of gray, face long and etched with deep wrinkles, sat quietly drumming his long fingers rhythmically on the small table before him. He waited for a response from the man with one eye seated at the table across from him. The second man, slightly shorter, a couple of years younger, also showing traces of graying hair, was weighing the question just put to him.

Jack Williams had heard the question before. Still, he was surprised it was before him again. This time the tone of the question was more emphatic

1966 was but a few weeks old.

On several occasions in the preceding weeks others, asking more out of curiosity, confronted him with the question. Would he run for governor of Arizona in the fall? This time, the man seated across the table from him in that small apartment at the Hotel Westward Ho in Phoenix, was U.S. Senator Paul Fannin.

Fannin's question was direct. "Will you run for governor?"

The answer would not come quickly, nor without much consideration.

Governor of Arizona!

Williams could never have known, more than half a century earlier, that such a responsibility might fall upon his shoulders. But certainly, few men in the state's history would be better suited to the task.

John Richard "Jack" Williams was born in Los Angeles, California, in 1909, to Laura LaCossette Williams and James Maurice Williams. Laura, knowing her son's birth was imminent, boarded a train in Ash Fork, Arizona, for the trip to Los Angeles. She should travel there, the couple decided, because medical facilities were almost non-existent in the tiny community of Ash Fork where she and her husband, a Wells, Fargo agent, were living at the time.

Before settling in Phoenix, the elder Williams' job would

take the family to Prescott, Arizona, and to Guaymas, Mexico, where they lived for a year. They might have stayed longer except for the revolution led by Pancho Villa which erupted through most of northern Mexico and included his seizure of the town of Guaymas. The Federales were brought in and Villa retreated. All foreign women and children, including Williams' wife and infant son, were put on the same train used to bring in the soldiers. They were transported to the border at Nogales. An American cavalry troop dispatched from Fort Huachuca met them. From there, Laura and her son traveled to El Paso. Her husband soon caught up with them after being shipped out from Guaymas to San Diego on a gunboat.

Wells, Fargo, forced to abandon its Mexican operations, offered Jack's father a job as general manager running its office

Jack Williams (1912 photo)

*Laura LaCossette Williams
and Jack*

*James Maurice Williams
and Jack*

in either Phoenix, Arizona, or Reno, Nevada. Since he had done earlier work in the state he chose the Phoenix assignment, moving his family there in 1913, a decision cementing Jack Williams' future into the broiling Arizona desert.

(Author's note: In 1916, American forces under the command of General John J. Pershing entered Mexico in pursuit of Pancho Villa, whose revolutionaries had been raiding U.S. border areas. On February 5, 1917, the Americans withdrew. Two months later the United States formally entered the war against Germany.

With the onset of war, the U.S. Railroad Administration acted to consolidate all of the nation's competing express companies. What emerged was the American Railway Express Company, with operations world wide. In 1928, a group of 86 U.S. railroads joined in the purchase of the American Railway Express creating the Railway Express Agency which operated its rail service until truck and airline competition drove it from existence in the 1960's.)

As a boy, Jack Williams endured more than his share of illnesses, the loss of an eye foremost among them.

It was 1914. He was in Los Angeles with his mother at the Hayward Hotel, visiting her relatives.

Jack suffered what he later described as a horrible, excruciating pain in his head. His mother, greatly alarmed, half carried, half dragged her son to a bathtub filled with warm water. Quickly putting him in the tub, she phoned the desk clerk who summoned an ambulance. The five year old boy, recalling the noise of the approaching siren, wondered how they would carry him on a fire engine. He knew nothing of ambulances.

At the hospital doctors probed and examined him. Their conclusion; a tumor behind the right eye must be removed immediately. The boy's father was not with them on this trip. Laura faced the agonizing decision alone. She agreed, the doctors would remove the eye.

Following surgery, the malignancy continued to spread. Doctors had more decisions to make.

They were aware of the visit to the United States by famed

French researcher/scientist Madame Marie Curie who was conducting a lecture tour, displaying her marvelous discovery—radium. She was also trying to acquire additional radium and financial support for her experiments. Jack's doctors were excited and curious about potential applications of the radium. Why not try it on the boy?

Madame Curie was approached. Yes, she would be delighted to share in another experimental use of the famous element which ultimately took her life. She loaned her pellet of radium to the doctors treating the boy. Along with the pellet came a guard to stand watch.

There had not been much research data compiled on the use of radium or its side-effects to that point. Doctors positioned the tiny radium pellet inside the boy's empty eye socket close to his brain. It was attached to a string taped to his cheek so it could be easily retrieved. Jack was told later the guard spent the night dozing off at his bedside.

Concerning the procedure Williams said, "Sober consideration of its use can only be viewed with awe. No measurements, no specific time limitations for its application, just an overnight exposure in the empty eye socket. Had the pellet been larger, had it been left in longer, who knows what might have happened? There was little scientific information available on the use of radium in 1914, and even less on its use as a means of curtailing cancerous growth."

Through the years, Williams wondered if Madame Curie ever learned what success her valuable discovery had in the treatment of his case. The use of the pellet that evening in Los Angeles, in the second decade of the twentieth century, saved his life.

Radium was the big new discovery in the world at the time. Uses for it appeared to be limitless. Among numerous other applications, it was used to create glowing numbers on the faces of clocks and watches. The women painting on the numbers frequently moistened the tips of the brushes they used by placing them in their mouths. Many of them ultimately died horrible deaths from the practice.

But the boy survived!

Through most of this century, beyond honors and recognition, Williams has experienced great responsibility as well. Little did mother and son know what the '20s would bring as doctors wrestled with the boy's eye problem.

After the radium experiment, other operations were attempted to enable the boy to wear a glass eye. All were failures. At one point he even took his glasses and glued carbon paper on the right side.

The missing eye would remain a focal point of self-designed humor and often unrelenting cruelty throughout much of Jack Williams' childhood.

The Williams family established several residences in Phoenix through the years. Among the earliest was one located about 16 blocks west of the downtown area almost in the shadow of the state capitol building.

The man who one day would be working under the capitol dome remembers the period fondly.

"It was the beginning of my youth after some serious illnesses. Looking back, it was a sort of halcyon period of going trick or treating on Halloween, and attending Boy Scout meetings at State Game Warden Joe Prochaska's home at 17th Avenue and Washington.

"It is from him I gained so much knowledge of virgin Arizona. He once took our whole troop to camp in the White Mountains—later to become one of my favorite haunts. We also encamped several times on a hill against which was thrust the Gillespie Dam on the Gila River, southwest of Buckeye. It was also a place, it seemed, upon which had settled all the rattlesnakes driven from the lowland!"

Jack Williams got his first job as a teen-ager hawking newspapers on a street corner in downtown Phoenix, buying them for two cents a copy, selling them for five cents a copy. Not a bad income for a youngsters' personal needs, but too soon, it would not be enough. By the time he turned fifteen, tragedy had struck the family.

His father died during the summer of 1924, just a couple of months before Jack's fifteenth birthday. Laura and her son faced a bleak future with no insurance funds and no wages coming in. It was necessary for him to get a better paying job.

The time for adolescence would be shoved aside, replaced by responsibility.

The Railway Express Agency, for which his father had worked, gave Jack a job loading trains at the depot located at 4th Avenue just south of Jackson in Phoenix. He had to get up at five in the morning to be at work an hour and a half later. He earned fifty cents an hour working a split shift of two hours in the morning, two more in the afternoon, seven days a week.

Fortunately for the slightly-built teenager, he quickly learned to employ the technique of leverage on his job. His assignment was to load huge quarters of beef, full cans of milk and other awkward and weighty items into the freight cars. He enjoyed the work and became adept at maneuvering the heavy cargo.

Jack's days were full. Between shifts at the train station, he attended school.

There were no child labor laws then. Everything he did would be illegal today, but the money he earned kept mother and son going.

Chapter Two

It's Elementary

Growing up in dusty Phoenix, Arizona, during the second decade of the 20th century brought many challenges for a youngster with a missing eye.

As a boy, Jack Williams endured relentless teasing from other kids. Many times the bigger boys would grab him and twist his arm. As they did so, they would demand he take out and show them his glass eye. Ultimately the glass eye was discarded when technicians successfully fashioned a pair of glasses for him to wear, the right lens glazed to block the view of the empty eye socket. He would remember people staring at the one-eyed little boy wearing the glasses with one frosted lens.

"In those days wearing glasses was seen as something only sissies did."

For the rest of his life, the single, frosted lens on his eyeglasses, would be like a badge of identification across Arizona, but an inferiority complex dogged him throughout his life; the missing eye influencing his thinking for years.

Of necessity, offsetting the complex, he developed a healthy sense of humor, an example of which surfaced one bright, sunny day in Santa Monica, California. He and his mother were visiting her relatives.

"I was riding my bike madly down the main drag with my head down. I rode smack into the rear of a parked car. About five women all wearing those big, old-fashioned floral print dresses and floppy, wide-brimmed hats emerged as one!

"They crowded around me, screaming in panicked voices, 'Oh, you poor little boy. Are you hurt?'

"No, I replied. But I lost my eye!

"One of the ladies fainted right on the spot.

"Well, we found my glass eye and the roiled waters were calmed."

Like millions of kids, Jack loved to swim in the ocean during summer visits with the California relatives. Because of insecurities about the empty eye socket, he would normally swim far off shore, in solitude, avoiding the crowds. He developed into a strong swimmer.

He enjoyed a sort of nomadic journey through five elementary schools in Phoenix, the city where he received all of his formal education. (It was at some point in these years he was tagged with the name "Jack". His mother's family had usually referred to him as "Ritchie".)

Laura Williams' success at property management and improvement was the reason he went from school to school. She would buy a house, do some fix-up, put in landscaping, then sell the property and move on to another. She was among early visionaries in the Salt River Valley, understanding that land values were sure to increase.

"There isn't an old neighborhood in Phoenix I haven't lived in at one time or another. We had three homes out near the state capitol; first on 17th Avenue, then on 18th Avenue and later at 1631 West Madison. I spent a lot of time roaming around the halls of the old Capitol building never dreaming one day I would be working there as governor.

"At one point, mother wound up with ten acres of land on Highland close to 16th Street."

The Year Of The Oatmeal Patch

Living "on the farm" at 16th Street and Highland, presented interesting problems to the family.

The accommodations were quite sparse.

A small shack had been erected on the property by attaching wood to the open legs supporting a huge water tower, forming walls for two rooms at ground level. A screened-in third room was fashioned above these.

A hammock, strung between two chinaberry trees, provided a cooling refuge for Jack.

"An outside privy was an important sanitary provision. Mom and dad didn't seem to mind these hardships. They were accustomed to them. Life was not idyllic as it had been downtown. But somehow, I managed getting to school and back."

The massive water tank hanging over their meager quarters provided some disastrous and expensive problems during their first summer on the Highland property.

Jack remembers at one point a strange smell developed.

"Mother blamed it on excessive sulfur in the water. As its taste and odor grew worse, we climbed up the tower to find a bird had died in the tank! This called for heroic measures. Men came to clean it out, and clean they did. It must have been a masterful job because when they had finished, and the pump was restarted, small drops of water began a persistent dripping onto the roof of our living quarters. The workmen had punched holes in the floor of the tank during their cleanup work.

"Someone made the ingenious suggestion to put OATMEAL into the tank to plug up the holes. So, my father unwisely poured in great quantities of the stuff. It was summer. It was hot. The oatmeal fermented, resulting in more foul tasting water and an even stronger odor! Somehow everything got straightened out."

But as he began his sophomore year at Phoenix Union High School, Jack's life took a dramatic turn and he would carry yet another personal burden.

His father, Jim, developed an ear infection and the virus would kill him in less than 24 hours.

"Medicine was not sophisticated in 1924. Vaccines were being used experimentally. Hearsay has it that a doctor took some of the drainage from the infected ear, made a serum and vaccinated dad with it. Whatever happened, he contracted spinal meningitis in its deadliest form. Father became incoherent so we took him to Good Samaritan Hospital. I stood at the foot of his bed watching him suffer ghastly seizures and convulsions. He was tied to the bed like a man on a medieval rack, his feet to the end, his arms and hands to the head. I watched him die!

"Just hours before he died, he had been quite stern with me and I felt much mistreated. To my eternal gratitude, something made me seek him out and say, 'Father, if I have offended you in anyway, I am truly sorry!' Those were the final words I said to him and the last time I saw him conscious."

Raising squabs (young pigeons) was among the family enterprises during this period. Each Saturday, Jack would take them to downtown Phoenix into the American Kitchen Restaurant run by Mr. Sing. Williams relates a story providing an early lesson he would draw upon for the rest of his life...the importance of clear communication between people.

When her husband died, Laura Williams decided to sell the farm property and move back into town.

The people who bought the farm, complete with pigeon coops, asked Jack, "What do you do with the squabs?"

"We sell them to Sing!"

"Oh!", came the response. "In Philadelphia, we sell them to eat!"

His mother received five thousand dollars for the Highland property. She and her son moved into a small bungalow at 17 West Wilshire Drive, closer to town, but still far enough out to have a Rural Mail delivery box.

Jack began working for the Railway Express Agency shortly after his father's death, working that split shift for fifty cents an hour. It provided a take home pay averaging $90 a month, or about $30 below what was considered a comfortable family income at that time. The Depression Years were nearing their end.

(Handling freight for Railway Express wasn't Jack's first exposure to the rail yard near 4th Avenue in downtown Phoenix. The family had been living west of the downtown area, only a few blocks north of a spur track, before moving out to the Highland property.)

During those times, and for the next 30 years or so, the railroads were the key means of conveying the nation's produce, including that of the Salt River Valley, from fields to markets all over the country. Mechanically refrigerated box cars would eventually replace those that were cooled with huge blocks of ice, but before that breakthrough, the "ice-cars" were irresistible draws for kids. Jack and his pals were among the dozens of other kids who would climb up on top of the cars, then descend into the big bins at either end of them where the ice was contained. They could grab chunks of the "white ice" to munch and enjoy the cooling it provided. The ice bins offered a cool shelter from the scorching desert summer.

(Author's note: The process of "icing" railroad cars is mentioned as an aside to illustrate how paths often crossed for many people as a small town grew up into a major city. Most of the ice put into those cars in the Valley of the Sun was manufactured by Crystal Ice & Cold Storage Co., a business begun by this writer's grandfather.

In addition to "white ice" used to refrigerate produce in the railroad cars, clear ice was supplied to thousands of homes in the Salt River Valley by the same company. The ice man would travel along the streets and alleys delivering his blocks of ice door to door. If a customer needed a delivery, a sign was displayed, and the route man, usually a big, husky fellow, would come in with 50 pounds or more on his shoulder and put it in the icebox. Those old iceboxes had drains and big pans under them that needed emptying each day to keep melting ice runoff from spilling out onto kitchen or pantry floors.

Other fresh food vendors would ply the dusty streets of Phoenix during those days selling door-to-door, too. In my neighborhood, I remember well the daily rounds made by a woman selling eggs out of a red wagon she pulled behind her.)

Williams' job at the train depot enabled him to attend school between shifts.

As pointed out earlier, Williams' elementary school years included a series of moves from place to place, never affording him time to establish many friendships. Instead, he often found his experiences in those schools full of persecution and fear.

It was during these pre-high school years he became a prodigious reader, mostly because of his confinement to bed or a wheel chair during various periods of illness. He read from Zane Grey and Plutarch and from authors in between; a wide spectrum of material, choices he would continue making throughout his life.

While at Adams School (later re-named Grace Court School) Williams began to establish some friendships especially when he joined the Scout troop headed by Game Warden Prochaska.

"Although now and then some of my fellow scouters made comments about the empty eye socket, especially when swimming and when my glasses were off, I found myself more and more accepted. After Boy Scout camp, came YMCA camp. Those were wonderful times."

Four years after World War One, Williams entered Phoenix Union High School.

Military training was still a required course for all the boys at Union. To be properly outfitted, Jack had to buy a uniform from the Army/Navy store complete with wrap leggings which almost always became "unwrapped" and trailed in the dirt behind him. He was issued an Army rifle fresh out of a crate, covered with gooey cosmoline, a material used to keep the weapon from rusting. The substance kept oozing from the stock of the rifle and despite his best efforts, he could never seem to get the thing completely clean. Being in the "military" class meant marching, rifle drill and exercise. Amid the ranks of young cadets, the one-eyed boy became unrecognized and almost anonymous.

(Phoenix Union's enrollment eventually reached more than five thousand, making it the largest high school student body west of the Mississippi River for a long time.)

In his new academic surroundings he became involved in student activities. Although it wasn't until he graduated, and started at Phoenix College, that his most prominent talents begin to shine.

Avery Olney, head of the English department at Phoenix Union, is credited by Williams for the "big push" toward a career in the public arena of broadcasting. It was Olney who suggested courses in public speaking and debate. As a junior, Jack won the state oratory championship held in Thatcher, Arizona. The subject of his speech, history would reveal, became a part of his life for decades. His topic for that contest; the dispute between

Arizona and California over allocation of Colorado River water.

Indeed, it was an issue not fully resolved for another half-century, one ultimately requiring a U.S. Supreme Court decision and Federal legislation to forge a solution.

But those events were long into the future.

In addition to attending school, Williams was working the seven day a week split shift for Railway Express.

In the late 1920's following high school, he became one of 250 students at Phoenix College, located, at the time, in a renovated private home in the downtown district. (Enrollment for the first semester of the 1993/1994 school year topped 12,100.)

Once in college, he left Railway Express and the taxing split-shift work he had known with that company in favor of other jobs.

He would earn thirty dollars a month writing publicity releases at the college often churning out five stories a day hoping one or more would "hit". He also filed newspapers and magazines and shelved books at the public library. He spent his Saturdays putting up cereal displays for the Kellogg Company in grocery store windows.

Income from those jobs offset the lost wages from the freight handling job, giving him more time to sleep in the mornings and more time to pursue a social life.

Of greater significance was the lesson woven deeply into the fabric of his character. By his mid-teen years, Jack was used to working long, hard hours. This solid work ethic influenced him greatly in future years and certainly was a key to his successes.

Still, a youthful Williams dreaded the process of seeking work, "Knowing the reason I was not hired for some jobs was because I had one eye."

One day he was hired as a radio announcer.

It was an ideal situation.

"No one could actually see me."

Williams' professional life in broadcasting began without fanfare while he was a student at Phoenix College in 1929. A notice was posted at the college. Radio station KOY was auditioning announcers. Jack applied and was hired.

Thus were sown the seeds of a full time career which opened doors to many places throughout the world. Through the years Williams became, quite literally, the "Voice of Arizona", especially after his friend and broadcasting contemporary, Howard Pyle, left KTAR radio to become a war correspondent during World War Two. Pyle later became administrative assistant to President Dwight D. Eisenhower.

For many years, it was Williams' voice that dominated the Arizona airwaves over KOY, and later the Arizona Network stations scattered throughout the state.

Jack Williams admits his insecurity over the empty eye socket kept him from ever feeling too important or taking too seriously, the prestige his talents in broadcasting brought him.

Chapter Three

Of Mikes And Men

"Return with us now to those thrilling days of yesteryear, when out of the past came the thundering hoof beats of the great horse Silver. The Lone Ranger rides again!"

"Look! Up in the sky! It's a bird, it's a plane, it's Superman!"

"Who knows what evil lurks in the hearts of men? The Shadow knows...eh...eh...eh!"

"Hennnnrrryyy! Henry Aldrich!" "Coming mother!"

Those phrases, and dozens of others, heralded the opening of programs during the heyday of radio. I have considered myself fortunate to have been born in time to listen, regularly, to most all of them. Thousands of American adults and children drew close to their radio receivers nightly to catch the latest installments of soap operas, dramas, variety shows, mysteries and shoot-'em-up serials. With the exception of those programs designed primarily for adult audiences or for the kids, people of all ages shared many wonderful hours together listening to the exploits of characters etched forever into our memories.

It was the Golden Age of broadcasting, before television began stealing our imaginations.

Today our busy schedules are often juggled to include time for watching favorite television programs. It was no different during radio's heyday. Families would gather in front of the console to hear the *Lux Radio Theater, The Jack Benny Show, Fibber McGee and Molly, The Great Gildersleeve, Burns and Allen* and *The Amos 'n Andy Show* among many others that were popular in the late 1930s and 1940s.

Television programs such as *Sesame Street, Mr. Rogers' Neighborhood, Shining Time Station, Square One Television,*

XuXa, Saved By The Bell and *Beverly Hills 90210* were still long into the future at the time my friends and I were arranging our youthful activities to accommodate the radio broadcast schedule of such programs as *The Lone Ranger, The Cisco Kid, The Green Hornet, Captain Midnight, The Shadow, Suspense,* and my personal favorite in the twilight of the golden age, *I Love A Mystery.* How I did enjoy the exploits of that daring trio of heroes, Jack, Doc and Reggie!

It is impossible to tell Jack Williams' story without visiting the early history of radio broadcasting in Phoenix. Both are inextricably bound.

In its infancy, radio broadcasting consisted of experimental/amateur operations, then commercially licensed stations operating with what must be described by today's standards as grossly primitive equipment.

People of outstanding character still dispute which of two stations, KOY or KTAR, actually was the first commercial radio station to broadcast in Phoenix. Semantics plays a role in the dialogue of this legend. Records of the Federal Communications Commission indicate the first experimental license for a station in Phoenix was issued in October of 1921 to Earl Nielsen for 6BBH. He operated the facility for a brief time out of his garage before locating it at 311 North Central Avenue at Nielsen Radio & Supply Co. Nielsen was granted a commercial license in 1922 with the call letters KDYW. Within a short time, the call was changed to KFCB which Nielsen said stood for "Kind Friends Come Back".

During this period, two brothers named McArthur were operating a car dealership while at the same time tinkering with a radio station using the call letters KFAD. That station, today identified by the call letters KTAR, was licensed commercially in June of 1922.

The McArthur brothers operated their station for just a few hours a day, frustrating Leon Black, a former gas station attendant for Standard Oil Company who saw potential in radio. The story goes that he approached the brothers asking them to extend the hours they operated their station. Black received an unexpected response. The McArthurs abruptly told

Black, "Oh, just take the station!"

He took it.

The Electrical Equipment Company, for which he worked as a salesman, was suddenly in the radio station business. Black ran it for several years before finally selling it to Charles A. Stauffer and W. Wesley Knorpp, owners of *The Arizona Republic* newspaper.

They built a studio for KFAD on the top floor of the Heard Building in downtown Phoenix. The location just happened to be on the same floor with the newspaper staff. The newspaper's presses were housed in the Heard basement. Soon after moving the station to the Heard Building, Stauffer and Knorpp were granted the call letters KTAR (Keep Taking The Arizona Republic).

Meanwhile, Nielsen continued operating from his Radio & Supply Co. store. He was selling and repairing wireless sets. Even before the calls KDYW or KFCB were assigned to Nielsen, he had a helper in his shop. A boy named Barry Goldwater.

Of his experience working for Nielsen at that time, Goldwater says, "I was in high school and I used to stop by after school to sweep and clean his shop. The first broadcast station ever built in Arizona was built there. We used a 20 watt transmitter. That's where I learned a lot about radio. They'd let me pour the solder lugs. I became, I think, the first disk jockey in the state and I used to play phonograph records and say, 'This is 6BBH testing', and name the record. I remember one night we got heard in Mesa. "

Jack Williams adds some of the history to this pioneering period in Phoenix radio.

"This was also the time when young boys were eagerly building crystal receiving sets trying to tap into the mysterious sounds traveling the air waves. Schematics for building the sets were sold for five cents, and Nielsen's store carried some components for those early receivers. By this time, he had expanded his business to include the sale of radios (Philcos and Atwater Kents). He also offered outboard engines and sporting goods equipment while continuing to provide repair facilities for the engines and radios. His expertise caught the attention of businessman Herb Stevenson, a man with little patience for radio. In 1927, Nielsen persuaded him to bankroll a new location for his business to a building across the street from the Westward Ho Hotel. In the basement of this new location, at 621 North Central Avenue, Nielsen put in a bowling alley. He also built a broadcast studio about the size of a small bedroom."

Soon after relocating in the new building, Nielsen dropped his experimental license for a regular commercial broadcast license and was assigned a frequency at 1390 on the AM band.

He was never happy with the four letter station identification. He applied for, and was granted, KOY which remain the station's call letters to this day. Nielsen began hiring advertising salesmen who received 20% commissions on air time they sold. In those formative years for radio, it was a tough ordeal persuading advertisers to buy air time.

Williams, after winning the KOY audition in 1929, began as a part-time announcer earning fifty cents an hour. Part-time became full-time following his graduation from the college a few months later. He read news and introduced records from the studios furnished in spartan-like manner with a few chairs, a piano and a carbon microphone that had to be tapped gently with a pencil from time to time to shake up the particles. A big window overlooking the sporting goods department provided the rookie announcer with a view. The engineer worked from a small cubicle at the rear of the building where repairs to radios and engines were done. It was a long distance from the tiny studio where Williams was broadcasting to the engineers' cubicle. He would scramble between the two locations carrying a typed copy of his music list, and the records themselves, back to the engineer to coordinate the programming.

His early ride in radio was a bumpy one, Jack describing his first day on the job as a riot.

"The young announcer, nervous and completely ignorant of his duties, had been instructed to go to Berryhill's Victor Record Store or the Brunswick Shop and borrow records to be played. For his shift the announcer would go into the studio, stand before a mike suspended on wire coils, tap the carbon center a bit to loosen it up and, when the light came on, would announce!

"That was it! He was to advertise Philcos. One problem! He didn't have the slightest idea that Philcos were radios. He does remember seeing advertisements of Philco batteries, however. So, on the air he went describing that moment at an intersection when the fire engine is roaring toward you and your car won't start because your batteries have failed!

There was no commercial copy, just off-the-cuff statements about the Philco battery. He ad libbed commercials for those batteries for two days before someone came in and said gently, Philco radios, not batteries! That was his first experience with radio announcing!"

The harsh reality of radio's capricious nature was impressed on the rookie announcer early in his career.

During his first summer at Nielsen's station, Jack was fired when Victor Guillard, a Shakespearian actor, came to town and was practically hired on the spot by the smitten owner. Nielsen could not justify employing two announcers on his staff back then.

As it turned out, Phoenix wasn't ready for Guillard's stilted British accent. He soon left KOY and headed down the two-lane highway to Tucson, a more cosmopolitan location of the time. There, he enjoyed a successful tenure and became a big hit.

Nielsen contacted Williams.

"Would you consider coming back to work full-time for me?", Nielsen asked. "I'll pay you $135 a month!"

It was a pivotal moment for Jack.

"I decided right then no matter what he paid me, no matter what hours I had to work (and I always worked seven days a week) I would accept the terms and adjust my own living to them.

"All went along quite well for a couple of years. However, Nielsen had a big load with the outboard engines, sporting goods, bowling alley and later, the acquisition of Brunswick and Decca records distributorships. Remember, this was during the depression. I truly believe the radio station itself prospered. As for the Nielsen Radio and Sporting Goods Company, generally, the bottom line was in the red!"

Just as the rest of the nation was struggling under the crushing burdens of "The Great Depression", Phoenix was experiencing its own economic trials.

Nielsen had already reduced Williams' monthly salary to $110 a month. But the salary knife was still being honed to a new degree of sharpness as Jack was to learn in another visit to his boss's office.

"Jack, I'm having trouble," Nielsen said. "We're losing money all over the place and I've got to cut your pay another fifty percent!"

That meant his bi-weekly paycheck would be in the neighborhood of $27.50. That was not a neighborhood Jack was eager to visit.

Stunned, he walked outside the building and had a brief cry.

Then, gathering himself, and remembering his personal pledge to adjust to whatever hand was dealt, he went back to Nielsen with a proposition; in his spare time, he would sell advertising spots or programs for a 5% commission while being allowed to keep the reduced salary already imposed. Nielsen agreed.

His first account was for a 15 minute program broadcast once a week called *The Seiberling Singers*. The time was purchased by Fred Tregaskas who operated the local Seiberling Tire store.

His next account literally walked through the door and onto his ledger.

It was on a Labor Day. Only Jack and his engineer were on duty when a man walked into the station and asked if it would be possible to "clear" 7:00 p.m., five days a week for an entire year. The fellow represented the nationally syndicated program *Chandu, The Magician,* sponsored by White King soap.

He told the man, "Yes, the time could be set aside."

The contract was signed, marking the largest deal the station had made up to that point. Other members of the sales staff were furious, claiming they had made numerous unsuccessful calls on the individual who walked in on Williams that day. They teamed up and demanded Jack's removal from sales.

Nielsen agreed and put him back on his original salary of $110.

Those years during the embryonic days of radio, programming firsts were the rule rather than the exception.

Throughout the country broadcasters were experimenting with formats and different programs. Live talent was considered the ultimate offering.

NBC was forming its Red and Blue networks, CBS had its single network and Mutual was also in business.

Under the programming hand of Jack Williams, KOY was

*Jack Williams at Roosevelt Dam (1941) reporting the
first time water went over the spillways.*

involved in its own experiments. Before Nielsen began paying for a phone line to Los Angeles to bring in CBS, Williams was already producing a program called *The K-Circle-Y Radio Rodeo,* an hour-long jamboree on Saturday nights. Here the cream of the local western bands performed for free on the street outside the Nielsen building. Residents were treated to the music of Charlie Munday, "Horsefly" English and his

One of the first portable recorders used at KOY.

Arizona Wranglers and Buster Fite and The Western Playboys who were brought in from Los Angeles. Fite soon moved to Phoenix and bought the Riverside Ballroom, on Central Avenue at the Salt River, where he began promoting his own shows as well as performances by other bands.

Williams could recount hundreds of wonderful radio anecdotes of course, many having to do with the trials and errors of those early remote broadcasts.

"Remote control broadcasts were difficult things to handle. We had very heavy equipment, including ranks of storage batteries, to lug around. When we decided upon the bold scheme of broadcasting high school football games live, I elected to do it from the sidelines. KTAR chose to broadcast from the top of Montgomery Stadium. It turned out they were right. I was dreadfully wrong! Sideline chatter is good, but the game is better reported from a higher perspective."

Among the most popular shows in Phoenix in the early days, were the remote broadcasts of The Old Time Fiddler contests from Woodlawn Park. Williams says that "Mom" Ruth would win contest after contest. But, now it can be revealed. There were no judges.

"I was the contest announcer and would circulate through the crowd listening to comments made as each contestant performed. Then, I would announce the winner as though a group of judges had been appointed, their names kept a secret."

"Mom" Ruth became known as the Champion Fiddler of Arizona.

Another program Jack initiated was called *The Sunday Afternoon Hodge Podge.*

"By now, the Brunswick Shop had gone under and KOY had both the Brunswick record franchise and a new record company, Decca, which was producing records with Bing Crosby as their major singing star. I had an unlimited choice of records to play, and persuaded one of the girls to answer phone requests. Thus I tied up my Sundays. It should have been a popular program, although NBC competition on the other station may have kept some listeners away. But we had the young people. This was long before *The Sunshine Hour* and Butler buying KOY and the magnificent years of excitement to follow.

"In those early days, during political campaigns, we also traveled around the state with the various candidates broadcasting their speeches. In Jerome one night Secretary of State Jim Kerby, who was campaigning for governor, was delayed down in Clarkdale. So, I tried to keep the crowd busy using the PA system which also happened to be our microphone for the remote broadcast. I would urge the crowd to applaud for no apparent reason, then quiet down...then applaud again. I did this just to kill time.

"Kerby finally arrived and, fumbling around in his pockets, stepped up to the open mike and shouted quite clearly, 'Where in the Hell is my speech?' His question was aired back to the Phoenix audience.

"During his first presidential campaign in 1932, New York Governor Franklin D. Roosevelt came to Phoenix to make a speech at the state capitol. A huge crowd gathered as a big, open touring car approached. Seated in the rear were Roosevelt and Arizona Governor George W. P. Hunt, walrus moustache and all! Someone from KTAR handed their mike to Governor Hunt who looked at it and exclaimed, 'I don't want this damn thing!' and passed it on across Roosevelt's lap into the crowd next to the car. KTAR lost their mike. I scrambled up on the rear of the touring car, over a couple of spare tires that were strapped on the back, and onto the folded top of the car. As I did so Roosevelt turned, looked at me and grinned that delightfully crooked grin of his. Encouraged, I held the mike up for Governor Hunt to speak into and then for Roosevelt to speak. I was so impressed by Roosevelt's warm attitude, I actually voted for him twice. And I was a Republican who had voted for Hoover!"

One of the most popular radio programs carried on the CBS Sunday evening schedule in 1938 was *Mercury Theater,* presenting a different drama each week. On October 30, 1938, the presentation was an adaptation of the H.G. Wells novel *The War of The Worlds.* The broadcast production starred a young, eccentric director/actor/writer, Orson Welles. Millions of people were terrified as they listened, believing the country was coming under siege by aliens. However, Phoenix listeners did not hear the Welles broadcast that evening. Despite the fact KOY was the CBS affiliate, and routinely carried the network's programming, that show was not aired then.

Williams says, "We delayed the program until the following Monday night by transcribing it onto huge round acetate platters. So, when the 'world was attacked' we didn't alarm Arizona as the rest of the country had been. We had the only existing copy of the broadcast outside of New York! In succeeding weeks we would pack up our gear and take that recording with us to play it for various civic organizations at their luncheons."

Just why KOY chose not to air the CBS broadcast that Sunday evening in 1938 isn't clear today.

Two locally produced programs had extremely long runs on KOY. One was Jack's own fifteen minute show *Yours Sincerely.* It ran for more than 35 years. (Its name was ultimately changed to *This 'n That.*) The other, *Rise 'n Shine,* survived about as long. Both programs aired five days a week, Monday through Friday.

One cold December morning in 1955, on his own program, Jack welcomed the newest host of *Rise 'n Shine* to the staff.

"Complete with ear muffs, clock, barometer, thermometer, coffee maker, and crystal ball...Len Ingebrigtsen has taken over KOY's *Rise 'n Shine* program. He actually joins our audience at six when Robert Capps, the southern flash, leaves off. Then at 6:15 comes *Rise 'n Shine*...the oldest morning program in Arizona. I can remember back to 1930, when Charlie Meighan ran the program, to 1933 when Eddie Calder, and yours truly alternated on it...Frank Weltmer, Paul Masterson, Dan Cubberly, Wendell Noble (later of NBC network fame), Steve Allen (YES, THAT STEVE ALLEN), George Graham, Bill Lester, Howard Black and Johnny Holiday, all took turns at hosting the program. Now comes Len Ingebrigtsen. Welcome, old boy! It's dark in the winter, but it's beautiful in the summer!"

(Author's note: *Rise 'n Shine* continued as a KOY programming fixture without interruption until dropped in a format change, following the sale of the station in the late '60s.)

Chapter Four

The Butler Did It!

"Block programming" was the format for a majority of radio stations throughout the country in the industry's first forty years. It simply means a period of time—15, 30, 60 minutes, perhaps longer, was blocked out for a specific program type. Such blocks might have constituted a news or sports report; a drama or comedy program; a variety show; or community billboard program. Even recorded music programs with a "host" would be blocked out on the days' programming schedule. In the main, the music programs were successful, but these were not the typical "disc jockey" programs of present day formats. Instead, they were highly produced, self-contained shows, featuring singers and musicians performing "live" before studio audiences.

KOY's programming was set up in "block" style. A fixture was the previously mentioned *Rise 'n Shine* program which aired 6:00 a.m.to 10:00 a.m. every weekday. The station also did re-creations of major league baseball games and Phoenix Union High School football games played out of town. Under Jack's programming leadership, the station built a solid reputation covering political campaigns, often following candidates on their swings to remote areas of the state. Those adventures were fraught with all the pitfalls such broadcasts would engender.

In the mid-1930's there were the daily noon hour broadcasts of *The Sunshine Hour.* Williams was responsible for writing and producing the hour long variety show originated from the cramped studio built into Nielsen's sporting goods store. Jack says the tiny studio, complete with velour drapes, was bearable in the winter months but stifling in the blistering heat of

Phoenix summers. Air conditioning had not yet surfaced to transform the desert city into an oasis.

"We had some amazing talent. I did have a habit of renaming the entertainers (I don't know why). My two most favorite names were for a girl singer, Patsy Prescott (real name Lela Hansen), and a cowboy singer named Fred Woolsey whom I renamed Pal O'Verde. A mulatto named Johnny Reddy was a great piano player. Audry Ingrahm became Marlene Ayers, Mavis Green became 'Sunshine Sally'. A male singer, I re-named Terry Donovan. We had a desperation system for rehearsals. A piano outside the studio provided music for each act. People were always rushing in and out the studio door. One day, one of the male singers rushing out to rehearse, hit an old cripple who fell over and broke his neck and died. But those were not the days of lawsuits and we kept the show going! I believe we used *When You're Smiling* as our theme song. The show opened with everybody in the cast singing it, then dispersing for rehearsals even as the show was on the air. Strange, through the years, I've never had anybody come up to me saying they once heard *TheSunshine Hour!* Artists performing on *The Sunshine Hour* received $2.50 a week and two passes to movies playing in town as compensation."

Another programming fixture of the time was the Saturday night *K-Circle-Y Radio Rodeo*. Williams wrote the skits and members of the station's small staff took roles in them.

"We were all experimenting and we had a free-hand to do it."

By 1937 both *The Sunshine Hour* and the *K-Circle-Y Radio Rodeo* were off the air and within a year the cast members had either taken other positions at the station or had vanished from the Phoenix radio scene. One of the station's most popular variety shows went on the air in 1938. It was called *The Gay 90's* with a segment called "The Meller Drammer." The program featured comedy, old songs and burlesque performed before a live studio audience on Monday nights.

One night during the re-creation of a Phoenix Union High School football game, Jack was in the studio receiving the Western Union ticker reports of the game's progress. Suddenly, the teletype keys tapped out the news that one of the Coyote players had been hurt and had died of his injuries. The player's parents were in the studio with Williams.

"I couldn't muster the courage to report it and just continued with my play-by-play re-creation of the game!"

At the time, his reportorial skills were not as hardened as those of some future reporters who seemed to delight in describing most dismal and grisly events.

(Author's note: Following the death of the player, a sign was erected at one end of the Coyotes football field at Montgomery Stadium. It read, simply, "Fight On!" Legend has it those were the last words spoken by the football player the night he died. The sign remained in place until the stadium was razed in the early 1980's to make way for new development in the downtown Phoenix area.)

As any listener to radio can attest, a certainty is the constant flushing out of personnel. Talent comes and goes almost as frequently as the seasons change. At KOY, while perhaps not quite as frequent, there were lots of those changes too. In the '30s and '40s, many people passed through the doors of KOY. Jack Williams was there from 1929 until he was elected governor in 1966. Williams' weekday programs did continue, however, through the end of his third term as governor.

"Radio broadcasting was once described as a loose trade.

"Now and then we hired an itinerant announcer. In those early days, some of them found trouble along the well worn path of wine, women and song. We had our groupies, flocks of young girls who hung around studios. Thus the drifters came by going from one job to another. Each of them added to the lore I was learning. One had a program he called *The Old Professor and His Twenty Brain Dusters.* It was an early version of trivia games so popular today. The Old Professor composed a list of twenty questions and asked them in an old man's voice and dialect and then gave the answers. I continued the program when he left. Tony Wons and his poetry program was popular, as was a show called *Between The Book Ends*—both of which I eventually copied for my own *Yours Sincerely* which consisted of all sorts of material, ranging from poems, to great readings, to special events. I ultimately changed the name from *Yours Sincerely* to *This 'n That,* more accurately reflecting its broad subject matter.

"It became obvious as years went by entertainers, first reluctant to appear on radio, found the medium a valuable tool in promoting their act. And advertisers also warmed to it as a way of selling their products. By the mid 1930s, radio became an established and accepted advertising medium."

One of the most successful national programs of the era, *The National Barn Dance,* originated from Chicago's radio station WLS and the Eighth Street Theater, each Saturday night. Headliners included "The Singing Cowboy" Gene Autry, Red Foley, Lulu Belle, The Maple City Four and Arizona's own Rex Allen. Later, during World War II, while stationed at nearby Luke Field west of Phoenix, Autry originated his *Melody Ranch* network program from KOY's studios.

Chicago entrepreneur, Burridge D. Butler, a self-made millionaire, bought WLS from Sears Roebuck and Company. He also bought a highly successful Midwestern farm publication called *The Prairie Farmer.* He began spending his winters in Phoenix as did so many others from the frigid Midwest and East.

Butler decided he wanted to repeat his Chicago success by putting together a farm paper and radio station operation in

Burridge D. Butler
Owner of KOY—1936-1948

Phoenix. In 1936, he bought KOY and pumped life into a paper called *The Arizona Farmer* edited by Ernie Douglas."

His purchase of KOY brought a new maturity to the station and Phoenix broadcasting, generally.

Jack Williams' destiny changed forever with the transaction.

Among other things, he began spending his summers in Chicago at the direction of Butler, who in later years was described by Williams as a sound friend, gruff, blunt and autocratic.

During his Chicago summers, Jack was to observe and learn the ways of operating a big time radio station which KOY was to become in future years.

"I was supposed to pick up pointers at WLS. However, staffers were so isolated, so specialized, that I knew more than most of them. I spent much of my time fooling around Chicago. By skimping on breakfasts and lunches, I could afford theater tickets to the great shows of the time."

Williams was assigned the job of driving Butler's car back and forth between Phoenix and Chicago, another reason to summer in Chicago.

"One time he had me drive his brother out to Arizona. We stopped at Fort Stockton, Texas, so I could send a sentimental telegram to my wife Vera because she had once taught school there. As we drove across some railroad tracks, a train showed up and our car's engine stalled. The car was demolished in the collision! The brother was unhurt. Butler never did reprimand me for that accident."

Several years after the incident, Jack and Vera were visiting friends in Fort Stockton. Vera asked if anything exciting had happened in the area.

"Well," came the response, "yes! One day two men, either drunk or crazy, drove in front of a train and wrecked their car."

Williams confessed his role in the event to his friends.

One of the first things Butler did after buying KOY was to buy an old arcade building at 840 N. Central Avenue, two blocks north of the previous location across from the Westward Ho Hotel. He then moved to acquire a more advantageous dial position for KOY. The frequency was moved from 1390...to 550 on the AM dial upon federal approval in 1938.

A remodeling program in the arcade building became an obsession. For many years, the arcade itself was unroofed. The studios and program offices were separated by an open air passageway, which in the summer was hot, and in the winter, cold—when it rained, wet! Two spacious, air conditioned studios were created. One of them housed a small Barton Theater Organ and Ralph Waldo Emerson, not the poet, was brought in from WLS to play it.

During the remodeling, Butler had to climb a ladder to get to his second floor office. The interior stairway had been demolished.

Among innovations brought to KOY from WLS by Butler...his announcers would all be required to stand up during their shifts. He believed if you were going into people's living rooms, you would stand to deliver your message. As the years passed, standing before "boom" microphones was abandoned as more newscasts were added to the daily schedule. The announcers were seated at the "news desk", the microphones positioned on top of the desk.

Butler's shrewdness in fiscal matters at KOY became apparent too. When his enterprises were making money, he ordered cutbacks in operating costs of 10%, which usually required laying off staffers. His managers would protest, but would make the cuts. Williams says the owner's pragmatic approach prepared KOY for the tough times that always came; the station, lean and trim, rode out many rough economic storms.

The purchase of 20 acres at 12th Street and Camelback Road in the late 1930's for a transmitter site was another example of Butler's foresight, according to Jack.

"He paid $10,000 for it and eventually sold off ten acres for $10,000, keeping the best frontage parcel along Camelback Road, which ultimately sold for $250,000 when I was running for governor and we had to bail out of everything to protect my ownership partners. My partners, at the time of the transac-

KOY transmitter building, 12th St. and Camelback Road.
(1938)

tion, were John Hogg's widow, and two men from Chicago who had been with Butler at WLS, Glenn Snyder and George Cook."

As maddening as it can sometimes become, it's expected the "on-air" talent in radio and television will come and go with gypsy-like frequency. It's a continuing texture of the industry given the understanding that it will forever be a medium responsive to public whims. The same nomadic tendency seldom occurs among staffers and management people who are not "on-air" talent.

Aside from some shifting and sorting through general managers, the management team at KOY remained relatively stable for decades following Butler's arrival.

Naylor Rogers from KHJ in Los Angeles, was Butler's first general manager. His stay was brief, then a mid-westerner took over.

Of him, Williams says, "He was a lecherous guy and frequently had girl problems, mostly with girls working at the radio station. The result was a blow-up in Butler's office one day and he was sent down the road."

The man did leave his mark, though. He is credited by Williams with one innovation that brought KOY financial security. Believing it would be difficult to obtain national advertising in a Phoenix market of 60 thousand people, he initiated the purchase of a station in Tucson, a market with another 40 thousand potential listeners. By programming the two stations almost identically he could offer those skeptical advertisers a one hundred thousand person audience base; the result was the Arizona Network which, at its peak years later, included eight radio stations throughout the state.

Captain Jack Reilly, a special events whiz from Chicago, came on board as the new general manager.

To many people he was a promotional genius. Among projects he developed under the Butler banner at KOY was what became a huge, annual 4th of July spectacular at the Encanto Park band shell. His most unique promotional gimmick, however, was a "Horse Banquet" held on the streets outside the KOY building. Prominent local horse owners were invited to bring their animals downtown to meet Gene Autry's famous horse "Champion". It was a major success among the local equestrian set.

Leaving Phoenix to serve in the military during World War II, Reilly did not return to Arizona. He went to work for Chicago Mayor Richard Daley as his Special Events Director. It was Reilly's idea, one time, to dye the Chicago River green as a St. Patrick's Day gimmick.

While it might have been perceived as a case of the revolving door for general managers at KOY through Butler's years of ownership, Williams continued at his post as Program Director.

It was not unusual to find him working at his desk well into the night, long after most other staffers had quit for the day. On one such occasion, the phone rang. It was Burridge Butler calling from Montgomery Stadium where he was watching a football game.

He said, "Jack, I need my overcoat. Will you get it for me?"

Of course, the answer was yes. Jack would simply go into Butler's office, grab the coat and drive over to the stadium which was only about a mile away and deliver the coat.

Not so fast, Jack!

The desired garment was not at the station. Instead it was hanging in a closet in Butler's home about 10 miles away at the base of Camelback Mountain. It took Williams almost as long to locate Butler at Montgomery Stadium as it did driving out to the house and back. But the mission was accomplished. The next day, he was rewarded with a new tuxedo, the first he had ever owned.

The new tuxedo didn't gather much dust. Jack was in demand as the announcer/host introducing many of the touring big bands that would hit Phoenix for Saturday night engagements at Riverside Ballroom or Sciots Auditorium.

These were times of growth and development for the young broadcaster as his experience grew under the guidance of Butler. Encouraged to participate in various local civic activities, he joined the Lions Club, Junior Chamber of Commerce (later to become its president), and the March of Dimes. He was local March of Dimes chairman at the time the Salk polio vaccine was first made available. He also helped organize "camp shows" for troops training in Arizona during World War II. The list of his community involvements grew to include membership and presidency of the Phoenix Elementary School Board, membership on the Phoenix City Council, Mayor of Phoenix and finally, governor of Arizona.

Burridge Butler died in 1948.

KOY honors owner Burridge Butler on occasion of his 80th birthday. L-R foreground, Jack Williams (mike in hand), Butler and John Hogg. Others unidentified.

After Reilly left for duty in World War II, long time Williams friend Albert Johnson, KOY's business manager, was elevated to general manager of the station. Johnson's father had been the first state treasurer in Arizona. The family was always active in the political arena. Johnson's run as general manager ended within a few years when his marriage fell apart and he left Phoenix.

The Williams/Johnson friendship extended back through their days in elementary school. In a manner of speaking the two had been in business together even before they were teamed at KOY.

We'd better let Jack tell the story.

"The 'Noble Experiment' followed World War I.

"The Prohibition Amendment was passed. A new age had dawned! Bootleggers, home brew and bathtub gin proliferated. Somehow it wasn't really breaking the law to produce alcoholic beverages in your own home! Nor were we unduly worried about visiting the various shacks in south Phoenix where beer could be had for fifty cents a bottle. It was the 'in' thing to do. And, happily, due to my high visibility as a radio broadcaster, I had entrée to the more elaborate establishments in Phoenix, too!

"Al LaTour's was the *ne plus ultra* of all of them! A huge old home, later known as the Red Wood Inn, was the perfect place for the high-stepping locals to gather. It afforded excellent privacy due to the dense growth of shrubbery and trees shielding the place from the curiosity seekers. LaTour served about every type of liquor found in the civilized world from 'gold vasser' to imported rums. The price was a little out of my reach, but now and then I dropped in to see the creme de la creme of Phoenix imbibing and 'breaking the law'.

"I had a wide circle of young lads who were close companions during these times, Al Johnson among them.

"The depression was on, and in Phoenix, as elsewhere, salaries were not high. But we were a small town and money wasn't always the measure of stature. Mom and I still lived outside the city limits, so we still had a rural delivery mailing address! And mom, bless her, gave me full rein.

"My pals and I formed the Heeza Pal Brewing Company. Pooling our money, we bought a crock, bottles, a bottle capper, yeast, and rubber tubing necessary to siphon the brew into the bottles then stashed all this equipment in the garage behind my house on Wilshire. We bought our supplies at the Malt Syrup Shop and for the most part, our brew came off in excellent bouquet and quality. Now and then we bottled too soon and found ourselves with a 'green' batch. Such product blew up or exploded when it got too hot. In order to avoid such a tragic turn, whenever we wound up with a 'green batch' everybody came over to 17 W. Wilshire to drink the brew while it was cold. We became a popular rendezvous on hot summer evenings and week-end afternoons, never considering what we were doing as breaking the law! It was cheaper than going to beer joints in south Phoenix, and more convenient. Had I been living under more normal circumstances it never would have been allowed, but mine were the exception; I was the guy with the 'safe house'.

"Everybody was doing it! Al Johnson's father produced a 'green batch' and Al graciously invited his friends in to get rid of it.

"Our group worked well together disposing of Johnson's premature brew during a busy afternoon.

"Unexpectedly, Al's father came home. One of the lads went to the front door and said, 'There's a funny looking little old guy coming up the walk, shall I let him in?'

"Al saw it was his dad. In he came to be shocked at the crowd in his home drinking his beer. He later claimed it was the best batch he'd ever turned out and his son had squandered it."

Another Williams contemporary of the day, Barry Goldwater also dabbled in some of the action, his recollection not nearly as positive as Jack's. "I used to make beer for my father. It was terrible beer. My mother would take us down to Nogales and buy a 5 gallon tin of alcohol. Once back home, she'd put it in the bathtub, mix it up with blueberries and make gin. It was terrible stuff."

In the early '40s, another radio station in Phoenix decided to experiment with a 30 minute locally produced radio drama, with a war theme.

Bill Lester was hired as one of the radio actors because, as he put it, he could read well. The dramas were written and directed by Paul Bennard.

With great self-assurance he encouraged his cast, saying, "Now remember, Jack Williams is going to listen to this and if we do a good job, he'll put us on KOY!"

It truly would have been a big deal at the time, according to Lester.

He remembers Williams did like the production and gave the group a half hour time slot in the evening for the continuing program.

Bill Lester's career at KOY was underway.

He had a marvelous voice, but beyond that, and truly unique to him, an ability to communicate with his listeners that was unmatched then or since. And he possessed a keen mind for the medium. Through the years spent toiling in the KOY vineyards, Lester climbed the ladder of success from rookie announcer to news anchor to program host to sales manager to the post of Vice-President for Programs, KOY. He would eventually become General Manager of KOOL-AM in Phoenix.

Lester first met Jack Williams many years before that radio drama crew was hired at KOY.

It was World Series time.

Will J. (Bill) Lester Jr.

Lester's father operated an insurance and real estate agency in a downtown office across the street from the Republic and Gazette newspaper building. On the outside of its building, the newspaper had put up a huge board displaying a baseball diamond. The animated re-creation of a particular day's game drew hundreds of spectators on the street below the huge board.

Lester says, "Jack would watch the board, then phone the radio station to provide updates on the games' progress. The phone he used was in my dad's office."

(Author's note: Despite what may be fashionable thinking in these latter years of the twentieth century, it was during World War II when women began to make inroads into "on-air" work in the field of broadcasting.

"Announcers were hard to keep in Phoenix, and elsewhere for that matter", Lester says, "because they would leave for bigger markets such as Los Angeles and the announcing jobs vacated by those who had been drafted into military service. As a result, some in the industry were suggesting women be hired as announcers.")

Williams is not restrained in his assessment of Bill Lester, saying he was "the best radio man in the business."

With his election as mayor of Phoenix in 1955, Williams' role in the daily operation of KOY was, of necessity, reduced. He says Lester became sort of an assistant general manager helping John Hogg with the sales department and guiding the programming department. In time, Lester would also develop a huge following with his own 15 minute daily program called *Top Of The Desk.*

Among the handful of radio stations operating in the Phoenix market area during the mid 1940's was KOOL-AM.

KOY was carrying CBS programming but that was about to change, as Williams recalls.

"CBS was raiding NBC and needed 8:30 Sunday nights (the hour held by Gene Autry). CBS wanted to put Jack Benny in that time slot. Autry told CBS he would give up his 8:30 slot IF the network would switch its affiliation to KOOL.

"My partners went to New York and waited.

"Reflecting back, it was really pathetic. I stayed in Phoenix to prepare our schedule for the possible loss of CBS programs. I removed all of the network's sustaining programs, their regularly scheduled shows, and just kept their commercials running. The favorable news out of New York never came. But we were ready. When the network decided to change stations we lost the commercials but there wasn't an abrupt switch in programming. We signed on with Mutual which carried, among its other highly rated programs, baseball's *Game Of The Day*.

"As it turned out, having exclusive rights to the *Game Of The Day* was a great attraction for us. Through some innovative sales ideas from Lester we used the change to great advantage. Over the following twelve months, our profits were up seventy percent. We may have lost some prestige in being dropped by CBS, but commercially it really paid off."

Chapter Five

The Boardroom

According to *The History Of Phoenix Elementary School District No. 1 1871-1983:*

"The roots of Phoenix Elementary School District No. 1 go deep in the annals of the Territory of Arizona. The first glimmering of the need for Education came when the Legislative Assembly met in the log cabin settlement of Prescott in 1864. (Territorial) Governor John N. Goodwin gave official recognition of this need when he stood before the delegates urging the establishment of a funded public school system. So the seed was sown, to flower when the third (Territorial) Governor, Anson P. K. Safford, prepared a school bill to be presented to the Legislative Assembly of 1871. As a result of his efforts, the school bill became law and classes were thereupon started in the town sites of Phoenix, Prescott and Tucson. Such was the genesis of the Phoenix Elementary School District, which was appropriately designated No. 1. It was officially created on May 15, 1871."[1]

In the early 1940's at the urging of Dr. Trevor Browne, a Phoenix pediatrician and member of the Phoenix Union High School Board of Education, Jack Williams ran for one of the three seats of the Phoenix Elementary School District Board of Education.

By this time his broadcasting career was well into its second decade.

His campaign for the school board was his first try for elective office. He lost, in part, because he didn't receive the support of the teachers union. Its influential leader, Frank Bradford, later told Williams his organization would have supported him had it known, sooner, he would be a candidate.

It would be the last election Jack would lose.

He found himself on the board anyway, having been appointed to replace someone who had been declared incompetent and was removed from the post.

Williams would go on to serve three consecutive terms as its president, before completing his service on the board.

The Phoenix Elementary School District was facing new pressures of curricula and growth when Jack signed on.

In Pasadena, California, a new theory in public education was beginning to surface. Labeled "permissive" education, some of its concepts and methods would rock the pillars of traditional teaching systems in large districts and small, all over the country. Embraced by the new approach was memorization as the most effective way to teach students to read. The old method, phonics, was to be discontinued. The famous *Dick And Jane Reader* was the popular new choice. "See Jane run." "See Dick run." "See Spot run." Those were some of the sentences championed in the new system's beginning reader material. In Phoenix, phonics versus memorization created wide divisions among teachers, administrators and parents.

Williams' opposition to the "permissive" camp quickly polarized teachers against him.

"I recall one woman counselor arguing with me in the office. She started crying. I told her, 'Look, if the world was remade exactly as you wanted it to be remade, you'd want to remake it all over the next day.' She was both distraught and furious."

Jack's tenure as board president was still fresh when he faced the threat of a teacher's strike.

"Teachers assembled one day to talk to me. Younger than most of those appearing before me, I looked into their faces and said, 'If you don't turn in your signed contracts before leaving this room, your tenure is ended!' Sure, it was a gamble, a ploy, and I was utterly wrong in my approach. But, they succumbed to my strong stance and the strike was averted."

With the turmoil of the "permissive" education debate and other hot issues of the day serving as a backdrop, the district was trying to recruit a new superintendent to run its 24 schools.

Frank Bradford had risen to the position of school principal in the district. He probably felt his was an inside track to the post of superintendent since his friendship with board president Williams reached all the way back to earlier times, when the two loaded freight together. And he did, indeed, deeply covet the job.

Here was another lightning rod issue for Williams. Two camps emerged in the search for a new superintendent; many supported Bradford, many believed the choice should be an individual outside the district. Williams acknowledged Bradford was certainly qualified for the post. And, he was a friend.

"I suppose I could have gone ahead and appointed Frank, but it would have contributed to overall turmoil in the district. Frank was a big, husky guy, with a strong personality. You either liked him or he rubbed you the wrong way. Our new superintendent had to have a diplomatic personality. With this in mind, I searched around and found Loren Vaughn Jr., the son of an old line Phoenix family, who had been working in the Bay area around San Francisco. He seemed an excellent choice, meeting both the outside and local criteria. (Vaughn was named Superintendent in February of 1951.)[2]

"The decision was a deep wound for Bradford. He was counting so much on the superintendent post. It wasn't long before he left his school principal's job, moved to Flagstaff and became a professor at Arizona State College, now known as Northern Arizona University. So perhaps it worked out best for him."

The death of Frank Bradford in the summer of 1991 at the age of 86, reminded Williams of some of the unpleasant personnel decisions he had to make in his public career...things he might not have wanted to do, but in his words, "were best under the circumstances."

Faith North served with Jack while he was president of the Phoenix Elementary School Board. She would later occupy a city council seat when Williams was Mayor of Phoenix.

One evening during a school board meeting, Mrs. North made a motion which was, in retrospect, for that period in Phoenix' history, quite progressive, or radical, depending upon one's point of view. North's proposal shook up a lot of people, white and black. She said the school district should eliminate segregation within its system. Board president Williams seconded her motion. The proposal carried two to one. The 24 elementary schools in Phoenix became unified. Black teachers were angry and nervous; many worried about job security and future hiring policies in a unified district. Williams assured the teachers their jobs were secure and the district would continue to keep the same quota of black teachers as existed at the time. Some white parents were distressed, for other reasons.

Williams remembers, "One white father, particularly enraged that under the new system his daughter would be attending an all black school, confronted me. I calmed him down quickly by announcing, 'Oh, just send her to any one of our 24 schools that you prefer!' In that moment surfaced the first blush of the open school enrollment doctrine now being so hotly debated."

Another rough personnel decision Williams had to make would come several years later, during his tenure as Phoenix mayor. Once more, it involved someone whose life had touched his.

Construction of a new city library was one of the major capitol improvement projects undertaken during Jack's first term as mayor. Officials wanted a new librarian in place to coincide with the opening of the new building. It meant replacing the woman who had been managing the Phoenix Carnegie Library for a long time.

"She had given me a job once upon a time, putting books, magazines and newspapers away. I felt deeply indebted to her. But she had no tolerance for reforms or upgrades in operational procedures. The woman sort of out-lasted tradition. No one knew what to do about her. Construction of a new city library was being planned for Central Avenue and McDowell. She wanted the job of running it and lobbied mightily.

"The Library Board reluctantly decided she must retire. Hell, she wasn't halfway willing to do that. She put up a real fight and it took the combined forces of the Library Board, the Mayor and City Council to allow her to go gracefully into retirement. I have always felt a bit of shame not championing her cause. I could have made the difference but, in my opinion, it would have held back library progress in Phoenix.

"Those are tough calls when you are in a leadership position. Friendship is important, but it should never blind one to facts of life."

Years later as governor, Williams had to sustain the dismissal of a former co-worker at KOY.

"Jake Higgins, sales manager at KOY, quit to run for the state legislature. After serving a term, he lost his next election. Arlo Woolery, head of the Arizona Department of Valuations, hired him. Jake insisted on hanging around the legislature instead of doing the job for which he was hired. Woolery fired him. Jake called me for help to get his job back at Valuations.

"I met with Arlo and asked him, 'Is there any chance of Jake coming back to the department?'

"He was adamant, 'Absolutely, no!'

"I was presented with quite a difficult decision since I had appointed Woolery to head the department. He served at my discretion, yet he was boss of his department. If I overturned Higgins' dismissal he would never have full reins of authority there.

"I looked at him and finally said, 'O.K., Jake goes!'"

Williams described those, and similar decisions, as "gut-wrenching". Believing they were correct, he says he'd make them again.

He certainly faced other hard decisions throughout his career as a broadcaster too, once rejecting a cowboy legend.

Gene Autry the "Singing Cowboy" of movies and recording fame, later the owner of the California Angels Baseball Club, had purchased KOOL radio in Phoenix. He called Jack asking him to take the job as general manager at KOOL. Citing his special loyalty to Burridge Butler, Jack turned Autry down. Such loyalty paid off when, years later, Williams wound up as one of the owners of KOY.

As Jack pointed out, "The wise and the foolish we do. And I guess it isn't the destination, but simply the journey with its many ups and downs, pitfalls, surprises and triumphs!"

After serving almost eight years on the school board, he resigned when appointed to the Phoenix City Council in early 1952.

He joined the council to complete the term of Harry Rosenzweig, a long time Phoenix resident and businessman who was on his way to becoming a major player in the state Republican party. Rosenzweig had to give up his seat on the council early in his second term, after moving into a new home located just outside the city limits.

Members of the council in 1952 were paid about $250 a month, but Williams didn't accept the money. Instead, he turned it over to charity.

"I gave it away because I didn't want to become dependent upon outside income and not be able to give it up if I wanted to quit. I did the same thing later when I was mayor with the salary of about $500 a month."

Jack Williams family. L-R; Jack, Nikki, Mic, Ric, Vera.

As a member of the council, Williams was reacquainted with the frustrations common to legislative positions. Even when public good is at stake, altruistic goals can be scuttled with precision by lawmakers, or city councilors, who fail to legislate with vision.

An example of the frustrations he encountered involved the failure to acquire water sources for rapidly growing Phoenix.

The city council was considering the purchase of several water companies from Spence Stewart who had come forward offering to sell. Williams and fellow councilman, Allen Rosenberg, liked the proposal. The other five members disagreed and the opportunity was missed.

Williams remembers those opposed to the proposal resisted primarily because, "They didn't want to make Stewart a millionaire!"

Jack felt the city had much more to gain from additional resources for water than any benefit which might accrue to a single individual in the transaction.

Angered by the council's refusal to approve the deal, Williams did not run for election on his own in November of 1953.

Within two years, reformers would seek him out again. A more successful campaign to acquire water resources would follow.

Chapter Six

The Mayor

This may seem like a bizarre statement to make, but Phoenix, Arizona, received a huge population boost because of World War II. Industrial plants for servicing the American war machine were established in the area. The Salt River Valley, including Phoenix, provided exceptional weather and terrain conditions for training military pilots; several flight training facilities were created as a result. Developments on the industrial and military fronts meant jobs, bringing thousands of new residents into the area during the early to mid 1940's. Fighter pilot training went on at Williams Field, southeast of Phoenix, and at Litchfield Naval Air Station and later at Luke Field west of the city. When the war ended thousands of those military people returned to the oasis they had found in the Arizona desert. Civilians who worked the war machine jobs stayed too.

The most influential leaders in post-war Phoenix, outside city hall's governing structure, were becoming alarmed at the negative side-effects of all the rapid growth.

Police and public health officials were being overwhelmed by increasing crime of every stripe, including prostitution and its accompanying diseases.

Bossism, cronyism and other forms of municipal corruption were apparent at city hall. Good ol' boys were everywhere in the years immediately following the war. Actions and relationships which might have been a common rule of municipal order in the major city's of the East and Midwest seemed to be gaining a foothold in Phoenix.

Local leaders watched as the problems mounted. The city's resources, perhaps even its will, were being swamped. Reforms would have to be made, reforms that would reach into every corner of the city's government operations from the mayor's office to water meter clerks.

In 1946 Ray Busey, a local businessman, was elected mayor on his promise to work for reforms. Within twelve months he appointed a committee composed of forty prominent citizens to study the city charter. They would recommend revisions to the charter to improve government. The committee researched other municipal systems around the nation, and after months of study, came back with several key suggestions. Among the recommendations, Phoenix must establish a "strong city manager" form of government, increase the size of the city commission from the present five members to seven, and change its name from commission to council. The review panel also recommended the mayor be one of the seven council members.

A special election was conducted in November of 1948. The voters were ready for change. The charter revision passed by a large majority.[3]

In July of 1949, a core group from the panel making the recommendations for change, set up what they called the Charter Government Committee. It was established as a nonpartisan group, selecting people from varied backgrounds and political affiliations to carry its banner in city elections held every two years.

The committee proved formidable. It's slate of candidates never lost a single council seat or the mayor's office over the next twenty years.

Not until Margaret Hance was elected in 1975 had a non-Charter mayoral candidate been elected. Six years earlier Ed Korrick, a Phoenix businessman backed by a group calling itself the Citizens Ticket, did break the Charter Government hold by winning a seat on the council. It was Hance's election as an independent which signed the death warrant for Charter Government. Never again would it be a significant force in city elections.[4]

Members of the city council ran at-large throughout city history until a district system was voted in by the people in the mid 1970's.

Almost two years had passed since Jack Williams left the

city council after completing the Rosenzweig term. Needing a strong candidate to head their ticket in the election of 1955, Charter Government (in the persons of former mayor Herb Askins, Harry Rosenzweig and Barry Goldwater) came knocking on Williams' door.

They told him Charter Government was going to announce its next mayoral candidate. Would he, as a news reporter, come to the Westward Ho Hotel to cover the announcement? Yes, he'd be there!

Williams sat at a long table with two dozen other people, many of them old friends.

"Each person got up and said there was only one guy who could win in the fall...etc. I listened but really paid little attention. Finally, all had spoken and a scrim was unrolled at the far end of the room. In huge letters it read: **JACK WILLIAMS FOR MAYOR!** I was shocked! I stuttered and stammered and muttered something about having to talk this over with my wife, Vera, who was in Texas visiting relatives. I would have to consult with her before giving them an answer. I thought to myself, I'm not qualified to head the city. The decision was delayed. But ultimately, I ran."

Goldwater remembers, "We told Jack we had spoken to all the people...(well, in truth, we hadn't) and we'd all decided he had to be mayor. By God, he didn't offer much of an argument. And he said he'd do it. He became a hell of a good mayor!"

Jack and his future wife, Vera May of Coleman, Texas, were introduced when she came to work at KOY as a receptionist in the '40s. She was a teacher and, during one summer break, had been advised to get some knowledge of radio broadcasting by Vierling Kersey, the Superintendent of Schools in Los Angeles. Vera was introduced to him while he was quail hunting in Arizona. Kersey wanted to put radio into his school system. He wanted Vera to be in charge of it, eventually. She went to work at KOY, never moving on to Los Angeles! Romance and marriage followed closely her arrival at KOY.

Vera was the perfect helpmate for Jack. Her sense of fashion and style, of grace and charm, her warm personality and ability to make people comfortable and at ease, made her a perfect First Lady for Arizona when the time came. In addition, she had an uncanny knack for remembering names, an invaluable skill which complemented Jack's self-described poor memory. In reflecting upon his good fortune in winning Vera's hand, Jack has often teased her saying, "You only married me because you knew I was going to be governor!"

A pre-election story in *The Arizona Republic* profiled first time Charter candidate Williams, saying the candidate was 46 years old, that his hair was short-cropped and showed signs of graying.

The article gave a brief sketch of Williams' radio career at KOY which by 1955 had spanned about a quarter century. It also pointed out what has been mentioned earlier, that his campaign for the mayor's job wasn't his first entry into the city's political arena. He had served out that one term on the city council in 1952-53.

The newspaper profile said, "The following year he was named Man of the Year by the Phoenix Advertising Club, capping a season of civic work that includes (his current) presidency of the elementary school district, activity with the Boy Scouts and Boys Club, and state chairmanship for the March of Dimes."[5]

Coincidentally, it was during Williams' tenure with the Arizona March of Dimes that both the Salk polio vaccine and Sabin oral polio vaccine were developed. Dramatic times indeed.

The profile also gave evidence of Williams' long recognized sense of humor and personal humility.

A couple of Williams' quotes in the article provide examples: "Phoenix has been sort of a two-way street. The city has helped and been good to me. And in return I've tried to help people here. If they think I can do the job, I'll pitch in and help smooth things out. Maybe I can help somebody."

And then there is this additional quote concerning his tireless efforts in civic work: "I enjoy all the civic work, but that's not the entire reason for getting into it. I think I can blame my old boss for telling me—'Nobody else will have you.' Maybe I'm afraid no other city will have me. So I just keep working hard for this one."[6]

Voter turnout in the three elections prior to the 1955 city election trended steadily downward from a high of slightly more than 53% in 1949, the first time Charter Government fielded a slate, to just over 33% in 1953.

The Arizona Republic, in an editorial a week before the general election in 1955 wrote about the declining city vote.

"Back in 1949 there were plenty of positive reasons for going to the polls. The voters were sick and tired of a city government which changed the city manager every six months. They were paying a city tax rate of $2.28 per $100 of assessed valuation. The city had few street signs and fewer street lights. Pavements were in bad shape. So the voters went to the polls in large numbers, and the first Charter Government ticket was swept into office. The new council hired a trained city manager and made him the administrative head of the city, retaining for itself only the functions of making policy.

"Under the three Charter Government councils the city tax rate has been cut to $1.75. Modern city government methods have been installed. The council has not played politics. Phoenix has won numerous awards for its street safety, its improved government, its efficient management. And so the voters have lost interest, as shown by the steadily declining percentage of registered votes cast."[7]

About 57,000 city residents were eligible to vote. Predictions about the turnout were less than encouraging as election day approached.

Voters would choose from four mayoral candidates; Jack Williams/Charter Government; Harold E. Whitney/Greater Phoenix Ticket; Sam S. Levitin, Taxpayers Ticket; Michael A. Parker/Independent.

The newspaper clearly approved of Williams, indicating such in an editorial four days before the election, "He is well prepared for the task of heading the council...it is difficult to imagine a candidate with a better background to assume the post of mayor."[8]

Some Candidate Commentary as the election drew near!

(Author's note: Jack Williams' daily radio program, *Yours Sincerely,* a fixture for decades on KOY, continued as the city election drew closer. As a reader of this biography you would surely be shortchanged if we failed to include some of his radio script material for your enjoyment.

A later chapter in this biography will consist entirely of Jack's radio scripts from some of his programs. Here are samples from a few scripts written around the time of the 1955 Phoenix mayoral election. Except for some slight editing for purposes of your reading comfort, the scripts are presented just as Jack wrote and broadcast them.)

(Monday, November 2, 1955)

"Lots of letters recently...One lady writes in, 'I'm going to vote for you for mayor...'. Another writes in, 'I'm not going to vote for you...you have too many things to do now'. That's a standoff!

Frankly I feel like a bird caught in a badminton game. I am caught in a battle of press releases. It's a new experience to Williams... But then, most of life has been a new experience to me... Each day... Some days I would not repeat, but there has been no day for which I have not been grateful.

My opponents in this recent race have been very nice to me up to now... And I thank them. Actually, this radio toughens you up you know—when you talk daily to thousands of people—you're apt to say things that don't meet with instant agreement. One of my severest critics was painter Oscar Stroble...whose vocabulary is exquisite. I have been criticized for suggesting people go to church, and for advocating many things I consider good. Because all people do not think alike...what seems logical to me...certainly seems illogical to another mind.

The thing I must remember, and you too, is that within the framework of this democracy of ours, there is room for all of us. The agree'rs and the dissenters. If the current press releases seem a bit bewildering to you, remember this, no two people can describe the same automobile wreck in the same manner.

"This running for office in a democracy, I can assure you, is an experience not to be forgotten easily. Even as nicely as I have been treated, the fact remains few average citizens want to get into the gladiatorial ring of politics and risk their hides. Too often, the professional gladiators must perform where citizens won't."

(The day before the election. Monday, November 7, 1955)

"Yes, in the Williams' family, this shall forever be remembered as the fall father ran for mayor.

All my working life it seems I have been exposed to politics. For 27 or so years, I have worked with politicians and reported political meetings. I have covered campaigns and waited for election returns.

I can remember helping George W.P. Hunt on the stage of the band stand at Library Park when he campaigned for governor. I have introduced Jim Kerby on the plaza at Jerome before 7,000 screaming democrats. I have walked the streets of Globe doing interviews for our *'I Vote For'* program. And I've covered council meetings when Dr. Reed Shupe and Bert Fleming, and Newell Stewart and Ray Busey and Nick Udall and others were mayor.

I have covered city politics when the city manager was shot and we rigged up a microphone from his death bed in St. Joseph's Hospital so he could utter the final plea to vote for his party. Incidentally, he did not die, and nobody ever found out who shot him in the leg.

I have had sinister bosses of Phoenix past call me on the phone and ask why we didn't include this or that in speeches! I have reported the first fist fights in the council chambers and in the mayor's office. It seems I should know something about this enterprise in which I am engaged. But, strangely enough, it is true. You never know anything until you experience it.

To have someone stand on an open platform and accuse you of 'arrogance and perfidy', and speak of your actions as being 'a stench and a stain on city government'; to have someone accuse you of plundering the city's treasury, brings a peculiar reaction. Of course, we understand the answers to all of the charges rest in the simple fact that 'it is politics'. But is it? Yes, I know political campaigns have always been conducted along those lines. And I suppose this one is better than many of the others. Good citizens offer themselves for office. And I suppose it is necessary they be hammered on some issues to test them, just as metal is tested on a forge for temper. Someone who cannot take it probably has no place in the rough arena of politics. No place for a dilettante or a sensitive person. I believe Spinoza has said no man ever knows a thing, really, until he has experienced it.

There is no conclusion to this morning's essay. If there could be a conclusion it should be held until after tomorrow. Tomorrow, the citizens of Phoenix will go to the polls to vote. So, those are the feelings of a guy named Williams running for mayor this morning."

(Election day, Tuesday, November 8, 1955)

"I have wondered if there comes any single moment in a baby's life when it realizes there are other human beings in the world? Or is it a gradual process? And do some babies never find out?

You see, I am one of those guys who is constantly amazed at how many different people there are in this world; and how utterly oblivious most of us are to the other fellow's interests.

This has been brought home to me many, many times recently in my job when I go out to cover an event and find thousands of people interested in an activity which I had never thought about.

Take last Saturday night...fifteen thousand at a football game at Arizona State; thousands more at a dog track; still other thousands at the Arizona State Fair.

No matter how broad your interests are, there comes a point where you run into something unfamiliar and consequently uninteresting to you.

For the past six months or so, I have been all wrapped up working on a political campaign. As the weeks have gone by, I have had to devote more and more time to it. As a result, I have missed going from one activity to another as has been my wont. I did not get to attend the solar energy meetings, or receptions. Just barely got a chance to take the kids to the exhibit. I didn't hear the Russians at the Press Club. I haven't been to the fair.

What has been so engrossing to me has been but a passing item of occasional interest to the average citizen, and has been utterly devoid of interest to others. Yesterday I talked to a friend at the airport who was somewhat concerned whether yesterday was election day. You know the type. Vaguely asking, 'Is today election day?' Really, almost absentmindedly.

...Today, of course is the day. And there will be many reasons why folks don't vote. I hope today there will be many more reasons why they will vote. ...Today's election can be decided by just one vote. If you don't cast yours, it will be the one deciding the issue.

I'd like to see a good vote for another reason. We have some visiting journalists in town. They're from a place where everybody has to vote, I understand. They think that's good. And it does produce about a 99% vote even though they have just one person to vote for.

They'd love to go back to their country and say they were in Phoenix during an election and in America, only 25% of the people or less, vote! Pretty devastating propaganda for the rest of the world. Let's get at least 50% this time."

(Wednesday, November 9, 1955)

(Author's note: When Williams prepared this script the morning after winning election as mayor he found on his desk a pamphlet from the Heard Museum of Anthropology in Phoenix. It included a picture of a shrunken head with the caption "Do you know how to shrink a human head?" Now to Williams' script.)

"Well, that started the morning off. I managed to get through most of the material on my desk and sort of clear the decks for action. But the shrunken head business still bothers me...

"I might add it's a pretty nervous feeling being elected mayor and if it ever happens to you I'll compare symptoms. I'm sure one of the head shrinking instructions would be to remember that only at the end of the term, not at the beginning, can it be determined whether you have been a good mayor or not."

(As noted, a later chapter of this book will consist entirely of Williams' radio scripts. Now, back to our story.)

Among the movies on Phoenix screens the week of the election were; "Shane" starring Alan Ladd, Van Heflen and Jack Palance; "Pete Kelly's Blues" starring Jack Webb; "Daddy Long Legs" starring Fred Astaire and Leslie Caron; and a film titled "The Phenix City Story" starring Richard Kiley, John McIntire and Kathryn Grant. It carried the admonition, "Cannot be told with kid gloves. Therefore not recommended for youngsters!" Another movie playing Phoenix the same week was "The Left Hand of God" starring Humphrey Bogart and Gene Tierney.

Postage for a first class letter was three cents.

Williams' victory was huge. He captured 67% of the vote and his six mates on the Charter Government ticket were also winners.

As for the overall turnout...doom sayers were wrong. The 1955 election brought out more voters than showed up two years earlier. Of course, the fact there were three full slates and an independent running, heightened interest.

Two years later, just under 33% of those eligible bothered to vote. They returned Jack to the mayor's office by another overwhelming margin. His opponent in 1957 was Rogers Lee who headed up the Democratic Charter Government ticket. He received 3,845 votes. The mayor received 17,128.

The Charter Government revisions of 1949 banned political party identification on city ballots. While post-revision elections were labeled "non-partisan" with Republicans, Democrats, and Independents included on Charter slates, make no mistake about it, Republican candidates did dominate those tickets through the years following revision.

Political analysts of the day said voter turnouts were dropping due to the continuing success of Charter Government Committee slates. It became difficult for their opponents to find candidates willing to make the race. The CGC win in 1957 marked its fifth consecutive election victory...without losing a single council seat. (The unbeaten string would continue up to the election of 1969.)

Following his victory in 1957, and with the support of major players in the Phoenix leadership structure, and of his Charter Government backed council, Williams embarked on what can only be described as the most intense, arduous campaign of his entire four years as mayor.

Convincing skeptical, territorially concerned residents in unincorporated areas adjacent to Phoenix that joining the city would be beneficial, took the new mayor into the community day after day...night after night. It was an equally tough sell to convince industrial operations outside the city to embrace annexation. Williams faced defensive audiences set on protecting their small community identities. The mayor's gift for communication and persuasion, coupled with his acknowledged personal integrity and honesty, proved irresistible.

The folks at city hall also prepared a film showing the service benefits a big city could provide.

"Once I began showing this film at the various meetings, challenges to our annexation proposals fell dramatically. In fact, it was quite a professional film and actually sold the deal much better than my verbal presentations."

One of the earliest annexations under Williams' guiding hand came in his first one hundred days in office. Phoenix grabbed about 5 square miles and 7,000 residents on the east side. Included was virtually all of Papago Park.

An article in *The Arizona Republic* reported the Phoenix City Council passed two ordinances taking effect immediately.

"The first ordinance met Scottsdale's annexation drive head on, encircling the bridgehead Scottsdale annexed two weeks ago. The second ordinance took in a long narrow corridor along the north side of Oak Street to connect Papago Park with the east city limits. Although Phoenix officials would not say so, the latter move was calculated to keep Scottsdale from annexing farther south and west.

"The move also brought Phoenix' city limits up against those of Tempe at the southeast corner of Papago Park. Mayor

Jack Williams immediately telephoned the mayor of Tempe to say that Phoenix has no territorial designs on the neighboring town."[9]

The expansion increased Phoenix to a land area of 35 square miles, more than double the city's size six years earlier.

A caution to Phoenix was sounded in an editorial three days after the east side annexation.

"How cities do grow these days! First Scottsdale, and then Phoenix! But what a shame that they should grow in such a haphazard manner.

"And yet we cannot blame the city of Phoenix very much for its latest annexation. As much as we disapprove of gerrymandering, the city's move seems to have been necessary for Phoenix to protect its citizens.

"Scottsdale's raid on the land north of Papago Park posed a definite threat. If it had continued on and annexed Papago Park, it might have destroyed forever the chance for the City of Phoenix to go into the area and construct a great recreation center for the people of the Valley. It would have removed forever the chance to move the state capitol to the Papago site. No one could believe Scottsdale, had it annexed the park, could have afforded to put in a golf course, other type of recreation areas and a stadium. No one doubts that Phoenix can do the job whenever legal difficulties regarding ownership of the land by the state and federal governments have been cleared away.

"The entire business of these annexations point, however, in but one direction. That is the need for projected cooperative planning for future annexation proceedings. If the area is to grow by a series of raids and counter-raids, the lost tribes of Israel won't be half as lost as the residents of I-Don't-Know-Where."[10]

Phoenix kept up its expansion push, this time to the Maryvale area on the west. Residents were ready to come in, but a major industry, the Reynolds Metals Plant on West Van Buren balked. Executives of the plant said they had significant problems because of city building codes they felt would create unworkable obstacles. Frank Snell, co-founder of a major law firm bearing his name and the lead attorney for Reynolds Metals, planned to file an injunction to block annexation.

Williams took his case to Bud Jacobson an attorney representing Reynolds, who asked, "Do you expect me to believe you will hold those petitions and not file them until we are satisfied with the codes?"

Jack promised he would. It was a handshake deal. He appointed a committee chaired by councilman Allen Rosenberg to study the building codes and make recommendations which would accommodate, not only the aluminum plant, but other industries down the line should similar objections arise.

Williams remembers a specific concern expressed by the Reynolds representatives.

"We learned that as a part of their daily operations, they moved huge pieces of equipment several times a day and our code would have required plumbing inspectors, and others, to go out to the plant every time something was moved. So, we fixed it."

Jacobson was satisfied with the code modifications and endorsed annexation. Maryvale was brought in.

Attorney Irving A. Jennings, Williams' long-time friend, controlled an area on the east side coveted by Phoenix for its next annexation phase. He said his area wanted no part of annexation and would establish a special fire protection district of its own.

"I went to him for some one on one jawboning, pleading, 'Aw, come on, Irv! We already have fire protection and can call upon a lot of different stations to help. We will provide police protection for your area and we'll fix up your streets and give you better water access!'

"Jennings paused for a moment, sighed heavily and said, 'O.K., Jack, we'll come in.'"

Along with aggressive annexations of these and other areas, including sections of south Phoenix, came the need to finance building the infrastructure. Another test of Williams' salesmanship was at hand. He had to convince citizens to buy into a $70 million dollar bond program, the biggest such undertaking in Phoenix history.

A bond committee was established to sell the proposal. The voters said yes!

Arizona State University history professor Bradford Luckingham, writing in 1989, said, "During the 1950's signs of growth appeared everywhere. The value of construction jumped from $22 million in 1955 to $94 million in 1960. There was more construction in Phoenix in 1959 than in all the years from 1914 to 1946 combined. *Time, Newsweek, U.S. News & World Report* and other national publications contained glowing stories of the economic and demographic explosion of the 1950's in Phoenix. So extensive was the annexation program that by 1960 approximately 75% of the people living in the city were residents of areas annexed.

"Phoenix increased its physical size from 17.1 square miles to 187.4 square miles and by 1960 the city limits reached 64th Street in Papago Park on the east, 67th Avenue on the west, South Mountain Park to the south and Cactus Road to the north.

"The annexation policy enabled the city to increase its physical size 11 fold, to about 187 square miles and its population four fold. (From 150,000 to approximately 450,000 by the time Williams left city hall.)

"In one operation in 1959, the city more than doubled in area and added over 100,000 people to its population. In the process it kept money in the city, greatly broadened the tax base and made it unnecessary to raise the property tax during the decade."[11]

Following his two terms as mayor, Jack and his wife, Vera, began to travel extensively.

They were guests of honor at a huge farewell luncheon. One of the gifts presented to the couple was a trip to Hawaii.

It didn't take long before the ex-mayor's life-long instincts as a reporter were brought to the fore.

"I hadn't realized how tired I was until a volcano erupted nearby and I thought, Williams, this is a great story! You should be covering it! I felt listless and morose. But I finally rented a plane and flew over the cauldron. I am glad now I did. It was night. Below us was a seething sea of crimson with a stem winding off the crest of the crater. Now and then huge explosions boiled its surface and great red blobs of magma were hurled into the sky. The wayward stem was actually lava flowing from a break in the rim. It plunged a scalding way down the slopes of the mountain, devouring everything in its path.

The Shah of Iran is welcomed to Phoenix by
Mayor Jack Williams.

When it reached the ocean a gigantic shroud of sulfur smoke and steam gushed skyward! It was a sight I am glad I saw and could report via telephone to KOY."

The return trip from Hawaii was quite memorable.

Their ship encountered a vicious storm preceded by a great wave. When the wave struck the ship, it immediately toppled and broke all the bottles at the bar, splintered furniture and frightened the passengers.

"The storm lasted for about 72 hours. Vera and I actually enjoyed the experience. The public rooms on board all had ropes tied across them providing something for passengers to cling to so they wouldn't fall down. Table cloths were wet down to keep dishes and glasses from sliding. But Vera and I would go out on deck and brave the storm, watching the waves strike the ship and break over the bow. From then on, we decided we liked ship travel."

Vera Williams, Arizona's First Lady
(1967-1975)

Chapter Seven

The Governor

During his four years as mayor of Phoenix, Williams had been away from his office at KOY more often than not. As he moved back into the daily flow of radio station business, it was apparent to him much had changed regarding the working relationship with his partner, and KOY's General Manager, John Hogg. Hogg's health was deteriorating. There were definite problems.

As an example, Hogg had hired a young man out of Yuma to program the station.

Influenced by the new man, Hogg began complaining about the music being played on the air. At the same time, Williams was expanding the station's news coverage. Always an avid newsman, he began "piggybacking" newscasts and commentary, one following the other. Had the concept succeeded, KOY would have become a "news and information station" in time. But it was not to be.

Hogg was tense. His demeanor defensive at almost every turn.

Remembering Hogg's father had died of a heart attack, Jack approached him one day saying, "You pick out any records you like and we'll play just the music you select."

Hogg replied angrily, "You're making fun of me!".

It became frustrating for Williams, recalling for the first time in his memory, he actually hated to go to work each morning.

In the fall of 1965, Jack was visiting with Senator Paul Fannin, R-Arizona. Fannin, himself a former governor of the state, asked Williams if he would consider running for governor. It wasn't the first time the question had been put to him.

"Ever since I had been mayor, Republican party leaders from Barry Goldwater to Clarence Buddington Kelland had asked me the same question. I had always said no! This time I said, 'Maybe!'. I went to Irv Jennings, my close friend and KOY's corporate attorney, seeking his input. He was really enthusiastic. Ben Arnold, chairman of the Arizona House Appropriations Committee, a man of considerable clout, also brought up the idea while we were attending a meeting at Lake Powell. Here was a prominent and powerful Democrat asking me to do the same thing.

"I thought, here might be a solution to the continuing rift

L-R; Senator Barry Goldwater, Governor Paul Fannin, Mayor Jack Williams.

between me and John Hogg. It seemed a good way out of the dilemma.

"I met again with Senator Fannin, He offered his unqualified support if I would run. I continued thinking about it.

"At the time, in our state's history, the political scene was completely controlled by Democrats. But I was a friend of all the politicians and everybody in the state knew me or of me. Should I decide to run, there could be great risk. To do so would surely split my friends, Republican and Democrat, right down the middle. My candidacy might create a real political civil war."

He was also concerned over the impact such a decision might have upon his wife and three children.

Finally, Jack agreed! Yes he would run for governor!

His prediction was right! His decision to enter the Republican primary drove a stake into the political heart of the party, initially. No less a political heavyweight than Barry Goldwater, the past and future senator, and 1964 GOP Presidential candidate, was openly critical of Williams' candidacy.

"The first questions Barry asked when I announced were, 'Why is he running?' and 'What's he ever done for the party?' Barry was not pleased having another Republican enter a primary campaign already pitting two long-time GOP loyalists against each other. Both were proven election winners and both had been active in the party."

The first relationship healed by his decision had nothing to do with the political arena. At KOY, Hogg and Williams were back on track with their professional roles and personal friendship. But in the spring of 1966, John Hogg died.

Fifty-six year old Jack Williams stepped out from behind the KOY microphone to which he had been married for 37 years, to begin his first campaign for statewide office. In later years he would admit to being almost sick with apprehension about what lay ahead.

One of the contributing factors to Jack's success in both his business and political careers was the ability to surround himself with the most capable people he could find.

"I was a delegator. Until someone let me down, I let them take on a job and handle it. If they failed, I reassigned them or let them go."

The technique was to prove highly effective as his campaign began.

First, he went to long time political strategist Stephen

Shadegg asking him to run the campaign. Shadegg knew how to get the job done. His impressive track record included successful campaigns for Barry Goldwater, among others.

Williams was put on a grueling schedule. By all forecasts, the GOP primary would be one of the toughest in state political annals. Jack would face two other Republicans: Arizona House Speaker John Haugh and Robert Pickrell who had been Attorney General of Arizona from 1961 through 1964.

The Democrats would also find themselves embroiled in a heated primary battle. Governor Sam Goddard squared off against two opponents in his primary: one a former Pima County Attorney, the other powerful House Speaker Jack Gilbert of Cochise County. Acrimony filled the Democrats' primary rhetoric. That group wound up shooting itself in the foot.

Williams found himself in somewhat hostile surroundings in the days and weeks immediately following his entry into the race, recalling many occasions when he'd stop in at the Phoenix Press Club people would drift away from him. Old friends who happened to be supporting the campaigns of Haugh or Pickrell didn't want any contact with the third man in the fray.

He carried his message relentlessly, barnstorming through all 14 counties, to every corner of the state from Douglas to Kingman, Yuma to Holbrook, flying everywhere in a plane provided by David Smith, a waste management company owner. His days began early and ended late. He routinely collapsed, exhausted, in bed; restless sleep, night after night, waking up a couple of hours before the alarm clock sounded its 5:00 reveille.

He would think, "Dear God, do I have to get up?" But off he'd go trumpeting his primary theme over and over.

"Give me a Republican legislature and we'll get the job done!

"I had not anticipated getting one. I was planning, if elected, to pursue the same plan a dear friend, Governor Sidney P. Osborn, had used more than 25 years earlier.

"He was at odds with his own Democratic legislature, thundering at them from his office, speaking sternly during his addresses. He would give them impossible tasks and then complain when they failed to do his will. He was one of our greatest governors. He liked me and in the latter years of his administration, I was recruited to read his speeches to the legislature when he came down with amyotrophic lateral sclerosis, commonly known as Lou Gherig's disease. The sickness eventually left him completely paralyzed. In the final months of his life he had to use a board with letters on it and a marker that he would move from letter to letter to communicate."

After winning the Republican primary, Williams quickly gained support from all the party faithful, Barry Goldwater included. Primary wounds had healed and ruffled feathers had been smoothed.

Goldwater acknowledged Williams' strength in the campaign saying, "Everybody knew him, primarily because of his management of KOY and his own radio programs."

Campaigning against Goddard in the general election proved a much easier task for Jack. The incumbent had spent two years creating a lot of tension between the executive branch and the legislature. He had a reputation as a man with an abrasive manner in his dealings with many in state government, particularly with the men and women upon whose shoulders fell the responsibility of writing laws. It wasn't unusual for him to charge into house and senate committee meetings to argue for something he wanted. (The practice was not one generally appreciated by lawmakers of the time.)

Goddard's campaign troubles extended beyond his disputes with lawmakers of his own party. His primary scars, baggage from a beleaguered Democratic party and ongoing scandals in the state liquor department, proved too much to save his job. He even lost a potential boost when President Lyndon Johnson canceled a brief stopover in Phoenix just days before the general election.

Goddard's campaign against Williams included charges his opponent was allied with the right wing, lacked compassion for the poor and was a "throwback to the Industrial Revolution."[12]

As Jack campaigned for a Republican legislature, he also articulated the need for reform of state government. For decades Arizona governors, Democrat and Republican, were at the mercy of their legislatures. The weakest link in the checks and balances chain was clearly the executive branch. Williams was determined to see it strengthened.

He also felt strongly the state was headed for big trouble in the form of increasing demands on the budget from public assistance welfare programs.

A political reporter for *The Arizona Republic*, writing eight days before the general election in 1966 said:

"Jack Williams...said yesterday, compassion for the poor ought not to blind citizens to the dangers of the welfare state becoming a permanent way of life."

The story continued, quoting Williams' remarks, "I think the only thing which has failed is the whole welfare system. Some people are becoming completely dependent on government. They are making it almost attractive not to enter the hurly-burly of our competitive system. They are encouraging the poor to lead sheltered lives and this is a crime. Everything we gained, we gained because we had to do it. I know what it is to be poor for I had to go to work at the age of 14. We must always be compassionate toward those who suffer and are helpless. We have the responsibility to see they are cared for. However...it is dangerous to substitute a welfare check for a paycheck."[13]

The day before the election, Williams' campaign committee ran a full page ad in *The Arizona Republic*, accompanied by an editor's note saying a 7 year old girl had sent a letter to the candidate asking, "Why don't you ever mention kids? Aren't kids important too? What will Arizona be like when I grow up?" Here was the candidate's response.

"Dear Elizabeth:

You must forgive me and other adults, my dear, for sometimes getting so wrapped up in the narrow, restricted land of the grownups that we forget it is a great, big, wide, wonderful world for children.

Why not mention kids? Why not, indeed, for they are what this campaign is all about. It seems to me, Elizabeth, the main purpose of the adult today is to build the foundation for a better tomorrow, for his children and the children throughout the ages. If we happen to build a better life for ourselves at the same time, then our mission is twice accomplished.

I stood a while ago on the campus of one of our great universities; and as I gazed at the magnificent buildings I thought: Here is a monument to our greatness. But that isn't right, Elizabeth, for a monument is a reflection on the past and our universities are great living things, just like the elementary school you attend.

State government is a living thing, too, or at least it should be. Just like your father directs your family with maturity and responsibility, so should the leaders of government conduct the affairs of state.

When you are given a fixed allowance, Elizabeth, you are taught that this is all you can spend; that when this is gone, there isn't any more. Government must operate the same way, or the dreams of our golden tomorrows will disappear in the tarnished fiscal irresponsibility today.

I know it is difficult for you to understand money matters at your age, Elizabeth, and it sometimes appears adults have the same problems—especially when they are handling money that came so easily through taxation.

When you want to do something that isn't good for you, then your parents say "no". There should be somebody to say "no" in state government, too, when the programs are not good for all the people. Government leaders can be delinquent, too, Elizabeth—and when that happens it is the people who suffer.

The rules made in government today will be your hopes for a better tomorrow; we are legislating for your generation, Elizabeth, and if we fail in our responsibilities, then we will be sending you unprepared into a troubled world not of your own making.

What will Arizona be like when you grow up?

I hope it will retain some of the pioneering spirit of

the past, for these were times of greatness for individuals.

I hope it will still be a land of bright promises and even brighter dreams, for we must move forward along the paths of progress or forever be mired in the forlorn fields of what might have been.

I hope government will be the servant, not the master, of the individual, for the flames of freedom have been fed on the fuel of individual rights for almost 200 years in our great nation.

I hope your Arizona will be one that still recognizes initiative and responsibility, for if we ever lose the desire to help ourselves, we will forever relinquish that responsibility to a welfare state more interested in statistics than in the individual.

I hope that you too, will be proud to stand up and say 'I'm an American; I am an Arizonan,' for when patriotism dies, so does liberty.

Kids are important to me, Elizabeth, because I am proud to be a father; whatever other honors might come to me, none will ever be more important.

Arizona is important to me, Elizabeth, because I have been privileged to spend most of my life here; I have been a part of a vigorous growing land and it has been a wonderful life.

You are important to me, Elizabeth, because you are Arizona; your generation must be given the chance, the opportunity for greatness.

God grant us the wisdom that we of my generation do not fail.

Sincerely,

Jack Williams"[14]

Election day. Tuesday, November 8, 1966.

These were the days of Haight-Ashbury in San Francisco and the "flower children", assaults on "the establishment", changing views on social and economic institutions, and the rising national angst caused by the growing U.S. military involvement in South Vietnam. (Just seven days before Williams' first inauguration, 385,000 U.S. troops were stationed in South Vietnam with another 93,000 either offshore or in Thailand.)

In Phoenix the first run movie theaters were showing, among other films, *"Dr. Zhivago", "Fantastic Voyage", "Harper"* starring Paul Newman, *"Kaleidoscope"* starring Warren Beatty, and *"The Sound Of Music"* starring Julie Andrews.

Election day weather forecasts were wrong. Instead of the predicted 80% chance for fair skies, snow and rain fell throughout the state. Still, voter turnout exceeded 60% and Williams' victory margin was more than 35,000 votes.

A post-election story in *The Arizona Republic* said, "Both candidates favored air pollution controls, a continuing industrial buildup, expanded tourism, honesty in government, a merit system for state employees and a strong state budgetary plan. Williams was more cautious about programs which would increase taxes. Goddard favored more spending for education but pledged repeal of the sales tax on prescription medicines."[15]

At 11 p.m. election night, Goddard conceded.

Jack, addressing the GOP faithful at their headquarters said, "It would appear the voters of Arizona have favored my candidacy. My sincere thanks. This is not a time for congratulations, but a time for dedication. We build for those who follow. I shall need your prayers for divine guidance and your faith and counsel."[16]

Williams' first decision following victory in his first statewide campaign proved to be one of his best. After consulting longtime friend and business partner Irv Jennings, he asked Clinton R. "Krim" Krimminger to join the new administration.

"My Chief of Staff, Krim Krimminger was the big secret for eight somewhat successful years, considering what has happened of late.

"Krim was amazing. He was the smartest, most astute, adept, hard-working and loyal man I've ever known.

"He started out in Kansas City fighting the Pendergast machine! He hung around airfields and learned how to fly. He became a Pan American Airways Clipper Captain, flying those lonely routes across the ocean past the point of no return. He had lots of layover time under the Pan American system using his spare time to go to school, studying at many universities around the world. He took law courses. He studied accounting. He became fluent in Spanish. He became a lawyer and a CPA. He came to the valley to attend the Graduate School of International Management in Glendale when it was known as the American Institute of Foreign Trade. He would later become a member of the school's board of directors.

"At one point, he was named receiver to handle the bankruptcy of Arizona Title Company."

Krimminger agreed to come in and assemble the staff. He signed on for six months, but would remain in the post for the entire eight years of the administration.

Jack would later reflect, "If I was a good governor, it was because Krimminger devoted eight years of his life to making me look good!"

Following the general election of 1966, Williams was exhausted. He and Vera flew to Houston to get some rest at the home of his sister-in-law.

The rest was beneficial but when the governor-elect returned to Phoenix he was nagged by doubts about being able to fill the job. But at least the administrative structure of his office was in place. Krimminger had done his initial job well. All was in place by Inauguration Day in January of 1967.

Let us note here Governor Williams was paid $27,500 a year. His Chief of Staff was paid $17,500. Those salaries did not change during his entire eight years as governor. Jack has always believed people working in those jobs should do so as a public service, not as a means of making money!

"I have always believed in the old Roman and Greek traditions of public service. In fact, I never took any public money until after my partner died and we sold KOY. I did accept the governor's salary. But, I paid my own way when attending Republican Governor's meetings. And no matter the circumstance...whenever Vera went with me anywhere, I always paid her way."

N. Y. Governor Nelson Rockefeller hitches a ride on a buggy with Governor and Mrs. Jack Williams during a break in a governors conference held in Wyoming.

(As an aside, more than 200 people on the state payroll in Arizona in 1991 received annual salaries of more than $100,000 each.)

As his transition group began moving in following the 1966 election, they found the Goddard people upset in defeat. Offices were stripped of everything including pens, pencils, pictures, even the furniture...everything! A spirit of cooperative changeover didn't exist.

Chief of Staff Krimminger provided a key piece of advice to his boss early on in their association. He called it the "headline test". How would an action by the governor look in newspaper headlines? Jack says he took the advice to heart and always did

Arizona Governor Jack Williams; Formal office, 9th floor of Administration Building.

Governor and Mrs. Williams arrive at the Inaugural Ball!
(January, 1967)

his best to make sure whatever he did in office, met the "headline test".

It wasn't long after the bunting and folding chairs of Inauguration Day were removed, before Governor Williams was taken to task by veteran newspaper reporter Ben Avery of *The Arizona Republic*. He questioned the propriety of a state-paid car and driver for the governor, telling him, "You have no right to that big car and driver!"

Williams replied, "But, Ben, every governor has had a car and a driver!"

"Yes, but there's no law."

"Well, I'll get one passed."

And he did. The bill enabled the Highway Patrol to furnish a car and driver to the governor, but, intentionally avoided state-paid transportation for Arizona's First Lady, Vera. But, the Highway Patrol was assigned responsibility for her safety. Whenever she went somewhere, one of the officers drove her car.

"Just before the election, Vera had purchased a nice home in the Encanto Park area only five miles from the capitol.

"After the election, because we lived so close to my office, I shunned riding in the limousine and drove myself to work.

"I was driving to the capitol one morning when I clipped the rear bumper on a guy's car. He was going fast. The door of his station wagon popped open and he fell out! I saw all this in horror. The driverless car careened on, narrowly missing him, then, crashing into a palm tree, disintegrated! I got out of my car and went over to the guy.

" 'You okay?' I asked.

" 'Oh, yeah.'

"Seeing his blood on the pavement, I said, 'You've cut yourself!'

" 'No, I fell on some wine bottles my son has been collecting for his scout troop.'

"I told him to stay put until the ambulance came.

"The story in the newspaper mentioned the wine bottles and I got off safely somehow.

"But, wouldn't you know, soon a police officer found his way to my office at the state capitol, and I was issued a ticket.

"From that day forward, I always let a highway patrolman drive me around in the car supplied by the state!"

There were other incidents.

One early on, involved a small bomb placed at the front door of the governor's Encanto area home.

It was never detonated, but it did alter living arrangements considerably. The First Family of Arizona sold its Encanto property and moved into a tight security high rise apartment tower on North Central Avenue. An officer from the highway patrol was stationed inside their home at all times until the relocation was completed.

When she wasn't away at Orme School or Prescott College, Jack and Vera's daughter, Nikki, would be home with the family.

She remembers it was difficult adjusting to life with security people around the house all the time.

"A couple of times before Mother and Father moved into the apartment, there were assassination scares while I was at home. Those times were creepy. Having officers prowling around angered me. Late one night when I crept into the kitchen for a snack, I made the mistake of not turning on the light and one of the officers scared the daylights out of me lunging out of the back hall. Just as he was about to grab me, I opened the refrigerator door and he saw in the light who it was."

Death threats angered Jack, too!

"I was governor during the Vietnam orgy. Many death threats were received. I got sick and tired of the threats and the constant surveillance that became a part of our daily life. One afternoon I arrived in my office to find all the blinds closed. I asked why?

'There's someone out in the park area threatening to shoot the governor!'

'Put 'em all up and let him shoot!' I said in exasperation."

Repeatedly during the campaign, Williams hammered home to the voters the necessity of providing him with a Republican legislature so he could get the job done. That is precisely what the electorate did. For the first time in state history...Republicans held control of the Arizona house and senate at the same time. When the dust had cleared, the lineup stood at 33 Republicans and 27 Democrats in the House and 16 Republicans and 14 Democrats in the Senate.

The first few years were a marvel of cooperation and change, as the Republican administration set about implementing its promised agenda.

Among the highest priorities for the new governor were two items; first, reorganizing state agencies and second, overhauling the state's tax structure.

Arizona's legislature in the '60s, didn't have much authority, the Governor even less, in terms of coping with a personnel heavy state bureaucracy which had evolved through the years. Dusting off an old study that had long laid dormant on a shelf (The Griffenhagen Report), the Republican leadership charted a course of restructuring state government.

Williams' first State of the State speech in January of 1967 addressed the need "to provide better services to the people, and to save tax dollars by eliminating duplication of functions."

Legislation through Williams' eight years in office created administrative departments within the executive branch including the Departments of Health, Transportation, Public Safety, Corrections, Economic Security and Environmental Quality. Also established was a Justice Planning Agency and a modernized State Water Commission. Revamped and modernized too, the Division of Emergency Services.

The governor was later to observe, "Bang...Bang...Bang! We passed laws creating these huge, later to be bloated, departments. But we also passed a civil service act freezing their employees into place.

"It was a legislature dazzling in its ability to act decisively.

"The moves changed forever the structure of Arizona's Cowboy Government. The only department we could not establish was that for Agriculture (later approved by another group). The newspapers referred to our sessions as the 'Gung Ho' legislature!

"Today, with hindsight, I am convinced we did more harm than good. But at the time, we saw effective change made in the state's administrative structure.

"Krimminger was the man to whom all department heads reported. (The way it is setup now, department heads report to subordinates within the governor's office. Those subordinates shepherd three departments each.) Krim did it all himself. With him handling the red pencil, we kept out of debt year after year. During one stretch of lower revenues, Krim got the idea of restricting travel among university personnel. The new rule mandated "one-person, one-meeting" which cut down the practice of large groups attending various seminars. He also convinced me to order all state travel be done at "coach" rates.

"We were tough. We never had a state budget deficit, always a surplus!"

In the years to follow, after Williams' three terms were over, researchers would confirm that holding state taxes down and making tax equalization a reality, were among the most significant achievements of his administration.

Robert Macon, special assistant to the governor, wrote in an unpublished 43 page summary of the Williams years, "Prior to 1967, when Williams took office, the tax system was unfair. Assessment values varied from county to county. Some persons and some businesses were over-taxed. Others did not pay their fair share."

In his message to the 28th Legislature in January of 1967, Williams said, "The main purpose of our reappraisal and reassessment program is to equalize property taxes for all citizens of Arizona, and to standardize assessment procedures in the future. It is not, and I repeat, it is not the intent of the program to increase tax revenue."

It was the governor's view the homeowner should be given all consideration, and the tax burden should lie principally where it could best be paid.

The legislature responded by ordering the actual value of each piece of property in Arizona be established, and by setting assessment rates for various classes of property, regardless of the county in which it is located.

In 1968, Ohio State was crowned the mythical national champion in college football and its coach, Woody Hayes, was named Coach of the Year. In major league baseball, Detroit beat St. Louis 4 games to 3 to win the World Series.

That same year, Arizona's state tax rate was $2.16 per $100 of assessed valuation. The tax rate by the end of the Williams administration six years later, had been lowered to seventy-five cents per $100.

The campaign of 1968 again found Williams running against Goddard. He won easily, carrying Maricopa County (which includes Phoenix) by 89,000 votes.

Former Arizona Congressman Sam Steiger, a Republican at the time of Williams' second gubernatorial election victory, doesn't entirely buy into the theories of some observers of the day that Jack was elected just because he was so widely known through his work at KOY. "You know, Howard Pyle was also a radio type, but he never instilled the same kind of confidence 'n stuff! I think Jack's radio personality certainly was an important factor, I think it probably helped. But, it would be unfair

The Williams Cabinet.

Standing L-R; Robert A. Jantzen, Dir., Game and Fish Dept., Wesley E. Steiner, Ex. Dir., Water Commission, L. E. Woodall, Exec. Coordinator, State Board of Regents, Col. James J. Hegarty, Dir., Dept. of Public Safety, Richard B. Howland, Dir., Dept. of Revenue, William J. May, Dir., Dept. of Economic Security, W. A. Ordway, Dir., Dept. of Transportation, C. R. Krimminger, Exec. Asst., Office of the Governor, Dr. James L. Schamadan, Dir., Dept. of Health Services.
Seated L-R; Dr. Weldon P. Shofstall, Superintendent of Public Instruction, Dept. of Education, John J. Moran, Dir., Dept. of Corrections, Governor Jack Williams, Raymond S. Long, Dir., Dept. of Administration, Albert N. Brown, Ex. Dir., State Justice Planning Agency.

to make it seem as if he wasn't a doer, 'cause he did fine. He probably was as effective as anybody. As governor, he was comfortable and confident. He was good!"

Steiger added, "One of Jack's great strengths, was, he was always the least self-important of any state leader we ever had. He was totally self-effacing and didn't demand any special fealty or anything. That always made it easy to work with him.

"The people Jack brought into his administration, Krimminger, and others, were all people everybody felt comfortable with. Maybe the key word in terms of describing Jack, both personally and as governor, would be comfortable."

Steiger also said Williams was blessed with a wife who, as First Lady of Arizona, brought great warmth and grace to the position. "She was very good at it!"

Before the election of 1970, the legislature established a four year term for governor. Williams would become the first person in the state's history to win election to a four year term .

While serving his state as governor he still managed to embrace his life-long love of radio broadcasting.

At KOY, there had been changes since he was elected to his first term. New ownership had taken over. By 1971, Gary Edens was the general manager.

He recalls his first encounter with Jack.

"When I became the manager of KOY, he wanted to meet me. There had been a couple of managers of KOY prior to my arrival on the scene that may not have appreciated the heritage of him and the station as much as I did. He has told me repeatedly he appreciated the fact I wanted to learn more about the heritage of KOY, what made it tick, its culture, etc. So he and I got along great right from the start.

"I think the first time we got together he said he'd come pick me up and take me to lunch! He came around to the back of the building in his chauffeur driven car. He was seated in the back of the car...and I sat in back with him. Here I am a 28 year old kid as the new manager of KOY, with a guy I hardly know...the governor of the state of Arizona...and we go to lunch over in the men's grill at the Phoenix Country Club. It was slightly intimidating. I'm the new trustee for a station he had been with for some 41 years and I'm in charge of the thing.

"So we go to lunch and I figure I'm gonna learn all about what it's like being governor. However, what he wanted to talk about was radio! As good a governor as he was, when he got with me he really didn't spend a lot of time talking about matters of state, but would talk about the radio station and his recollections of the way things were...what a struggle it was particularly during the '30s to keep the station on the air and how they literally lived from paycheck to paycheck in the early days of Phoenix. It's a wonder that KOY even made it through the '30s.

"But he talked a lot about that...about some concerns over the growing number of radio stations and how it was difficult for the old ways of broadcasting to continue due to so much competition.

"At that time we had to become more specialized. We continued to do a good job in news but we also began playing the more popular music of the day. I always felt it was my job to explain to Governor Jack what we were doing at KOY, the changes being made in our approach and format, because we were sort of a popular music station, not a top 40 station, but certainly more contemporary in our musical approach than we were when he was here on a daily basis. He probably didn't relate to all the music. I mean we were playing The Beatles and the other popular groups. He was probably wondering whatever happened to Peggy Lee, Tony Bennett and Frank Sinatra, which ironically enough we now play (in 1993), but we didn't at that time."

As Governor of Arizona, Williams continued to broadcast his program *Yours Sincerely.*

The way he went about that task made a lasting impression on Edens.

"He would usually come in once a week to tape the programs. And what struck me was here was the governor of the state who would come in on Saturdays, usually. He still had a key to the station and he'd come in the back door and go into one of the production studios, setup his own tape, work his own board, and sit down and read a script that he had personally typed. So I was impressed with the fact that here is a radio man on the weekends...not so much a governor.

"That which he would talk about in those programs didn't always deal with matters of state—many times it did, but he did not do the show in his capacity as governor. He did it as a radio personality. What struck me was that he had been heard on KOY since 1929. Even though he was elected governor in 1966, he continued to want to do that program, even when the radio station was sold to some people back in North Carolina, he made sure his arrangement was, 'Okay, I still want to be identified with KOY'.

"As I recall what happened, because he was governor, it was felt by the ownership of KOY at the time, and I'm sure Governor Jack, that his program should be made available to any station

Gary Edens, President of KOY

that would want to run it because he was the governor. But the actual master recordings were made here (at KOY) and then anybody that wanted dubs could get them. So his show actually was heard on several stations in addition to ours.

"He was heard on KOY as a radio personality (not called that in 1929 of course...the medium was so young) consecutively from 1929 through 1974. His name became a household word throughout Arizona. And of course, one thing that made his show so distinctive is the way he opened it. He would start each program by saying, 'It's another beautiful day in Arizona, leave us all enjoy it.' That phrase drove the English teachers crazy. It became his signature!

"I was struck by the fact that here's this man, the Governor of Arizona, who acted like a regular guy, I thought. He came down on Saturdays, recorded his show like any other newsman or personality at the time. He didn't, because he was governor, require engineers or want to put anybody out or expect to be treated any differently than anybody else."

The 1970 gubernatorial campaign proved to be Jack Williams' toughest.

Raul Castro, a former Pima County Superior Court Judge, who would eventually become U.S. Ambassador to two Latin American countries, carried the Democratic party banner into the campaign and proved a most formidable opponent. Only a 36,811 vote margin in Maricopa County turned the tide for the governor, providing the boost needed for re-election. Castro captured much of rural Arizona and beat Williams handily in the Democratic promise land of Pima County. His vote margin there was 22,495. The final statewide tally showed the incumbent won by 7,406 votes.

Castro was elected governor in November of 1974 and served two years and ten months of his four year term. He resigned to accept an ambassadorship.

In an editorial following Williams' third election, *The Arizona Republic* said, "...for some five hours after the polls had closed, Democratic candidate Raul Castro from Tucson was ahead in the tabulations. It was only when the massive voting totals from Maricopa County came in that the Republicans began to breathe easily again.

"Jack Williams has been a good governor. There was nothing in his record that his opponents could make capital out of. He has managed to get along with the legislature, despite his party's razor-thin majority. Now he will have four years to advance the programs that he has initiated since his first election in 1966."[17]

Throughout his three terms as governor he championed the virtues of prudence and economy in spending the taxpayers' money. But Williams' tough fiscal policies began to seriously erode his popularity within his own party leadership in the legislature. The executive and legislative branches began to quarrel.

In 1971, the governor told lawmakers, "Frugality is a virtue seldom appreciated, but it has been the cornerstone of this state's success in maintaining solvency and a relatively reasonable tax structure. This state is debt-free and on a cash basis. Let us stay that way. Let us not be ashamed if we do not spend all of the money we can collect from the taxpayers. Let us remember that they, too, deserve consideration."

Arguably the most influential man in the legislature at the time was House Majority Leader Burton Barr, a fellow Republican.

"He and I didn't see things the same way anymore. (However, later I campaigned for him when he ran for governor). But the legislature was always seeking more power.

"State governors routinely are offered scores of free trips (junkets, they're called). I took only one during my eight years in office. My last year, after announcing I would not run for another term, I took a trip to Japan with Vera as guests of the Japanese government. It was very high level. Vera met with the Queen and I met personally with the Emperor, Hirohito.

"But while I was gone, the legislature decided they wanted more control over the new departments they had created. So, they drew laws giving them authority to set salaries for the directors of those departments. And they did this while I was out of the country.

"Burt Barr came into my office asking, 'Governor, are you going to veto these bills?'

"You're damned right I am and I'll veto every other God-damned bill you pass, and you can stay in session all summer over-riding my vetoes!'"

"Saying nothing, Burt rose and left my office, returning to his own. Those bills died in committee."

Water has been the key to growth and prosperity in the Salt River Valley since the days the Hohokam ditches and canals carried water around the valley ultimately to become the town-site of Phoenix several centuries later. This was long before Jack Swilling came upon the scene following the Civil War.

Arizona citizens from all walks of life have lent their considerable talents to the pursuit of finding adequate water resources. Politicians, business and agricultural leaders, lawyers and others invested much of their lives to that end. In truth, for most all of the 20th century there has been, for Arizona, a constant quest for those resources.

A group of people under the chairmanship of a future U.S. President, Herbert Hoover, and including then Arizona Water Commissioner W. S. Norviel, met in Santa Fe, New Mexico, in 1922 to draw up what became known as the Colorado River Compact. Six states in addition to Arizona were represented. Those six signed on in 1923. It would not be until 1944 before Arizona's legislature ratified its consent to the terms of the compact.

In 1947 Senator Ernest McFarland, D-Arizona, sponsored

Senate Bill 1175. It was the enabling measure creating the Central Arizona Project, the canal needed to transport water to central Arizona from the Colorado River.

It would take massive funding from the federal government to make the plan a reality.

Twenty-one years later, despite intense opposition from California, the Central Arizona Project received final authorization thanks to the herculean persistence of various members of the state's small, but influential, congressional delegation. Leading the effort for most of the twenty years it took to gain

U. S. Interior Secretary, Rogers Morton and Governor Jack Williams at Colorado River site of CAP construction. They are detonating the first charge of dynamite to start the project.

approval were, among others, Arizona's U.S. Senators Carl Hayden, Barry Goldwater and Paul Fannin and Congressmen John Rhodes, Sam Steiger and Morris Udall.

At an estimated cost of three-and-a-half billion dollars, the Central Arizona Project became the largest project ever undertaken by the U.S. Bureau of Reclamation.

(Author's note: Final cost estimates, and repayment issues, continued making headlines as recently as December, 1993.)

Five years before federal authorization of the CAP, the U.S. Supreme Court ruled, in an historic decision, Arizona was entitled to 2.8 million acre feet of water from the Colorado.

Governor Williams signed the formal contract with the Bureau of Reclamation for construction of the 335-mile-long canal; an intriguing moment for him since he, with the others, had lobbied for years on behalf of the project both in his role as governor and when he was mayor of Phoenix.

Earlier we noted Jack (as a junior in high school in 1924) had won a state debate contest on the subject of the dispute between Arizona and California over allocation of Colorado River water.

Sam Steiger, late in 1993, said although Governor Williams went to Washington to do "the ritual testimony on the project" it was very much a congressional deal.

"It wasn't a gubernatorial deal. Senator Carl Hayden was chairman of the Senate Appropriations Committee at the time and that's what enabled the project to go through. They can talk about all the statesmanship they want to, but Hayden just blackmailed it through!"

Today, Steiger says of his participation in the legislation, "It was one of the worst votes I ever made. Absolutely, it was worse than a boondoggle. It was a rape at the time. And today, we are wondering how we're gonna pay for it!"

Following his three terms as governor, Williams was elected a member of the board of directors for the Central Arizona Water Conservation District. He later became its president. The district's mission is to administer water allocation and repayment of the debt for the Central Arizona Project.

At this writing, Jack remains committed to efforts in search of additional sources of water for his Arizona. He openly favors a proposal by the North America Water and Power Alliance to bring water from Alaska down through Canada into the United States desert southwest and on into Mexico.

Whether such a project could ever gain approval and become reality will be left to future historians to note.

Barry Goldwater, interviewed for this book, was asked to describe Jack Williams and his service to both Phoenix and the state of Arizona.

Goldwater said, "He's a perfect gentleman. One of the best citizens we've ever had living in this state. He is terribly quiet. To talk with him, you'd never know he was a mayor or governor. Jack is tremendously well-read, informed." And he added, "He has always had a marvelous ability to get people to work together. People ask me why I liked Dwight Eisenhower! That's my answer. I say he could get people together. Jack could do the same thing. He was the first governor, even the first mayor we had who could get Tucson and Phoenix to talk with each other, Tucson being so liberal, and Phoenix so conservative."

Chapter Eight

Tempests In The Spotlight

Integrity. Honesty. Responsibility. Bulldog tenacity. And, NO personal agenda. Those were the qualities Jack Williams brought to his role as Arizona's chief executive. No man in the office before, or since, could match his skill at communicating with the legislature or with the citizens. Communication, after all, had been Williams' entire life since his first day in radio back in 1929. Voters in Arizona knew just about all there was to know of the man when he ran for governor the first time in 1966. He could not have spent so many years in broadcasting, especially with his own daily program as a forum, without "coming clean" as both a public and private person. It became apparent early in his initial statewide campaign people in every corner of Arizona knew of him, and were openly generous in their expressed support and trust. In candidate Jack Williams, the people knew what they were getting. Even his opponents, and their supporters, found it difficult to square off against the man personally.

The early years of Williams' administration were marvels of cooperation and efficiency in terms of managing state affairs and getting legislative programs adopted. He could point with justified pride to the significant achievement of budget sanity throughout his entire eight years in office. There were always surplus funds in the state treasury at the conclusion of each fiscal year under his leadership.

The reality of politics being what it is, those governed eventually start to grumble, start looking for clay feet on their leaders.

It would be wrong to conclude Williams' eight year tenure was untouched by controversy. Certainly there were unsettling issues, particularly as he entered his third term...his final four years in office.

Prominent among those was a recall drive, begun after he signed a new farm labor bill in May of 1972.

THE RECALL THAT DIDN'T HAPPEN!

In 1965, a Mexican-American farm worker named Cesar Chavez was beginning a campaign to organize migrant workers in the San Joaquin Valley of California. The initial target of his drive was the table grape industry. It wasn't long before the lettuce and melon fields of the Imperial Valley in California and the Yuma and Salt River Valleys of Arizona became targets of his activist crusade.

His tactics of demonstrations, strikes, and boycotts gained him victories, detractors and national attention.

Liberals and social reformers championed his efforts. Conservatives, farm bureaus, and even some labor unions waged opposition in forums far and wide. Heavy hitters of the day in the Democratic party turned out in high profile support of Chavez' passionate efforts at rallies in California and before congressional hearings in Washington.

Arizona's legislature had been lobbied mightily by farmers for passage of a labor bill to protect their interests against the Chavez organizing groundswell. It would ban secondary boycotts, allow growers to seek 10 day restraining orders against any strikes at harvest time and establish procedures for a mediation board in agriculture disputes.

Violence between members of the Teamsters Union and Chavez' United Farm Workers in some cantaloupe fields in the Yuma area sparked rapid passage of the bill.

Ronald Taylor's book *Chavez and the Farm Workers* chronicled the United Farm Workers Organizing Committee efforts with emphasis on its work in California and Oregon.

According to Taylor, Arizona was another matter.

"This was a right-to-work state, under section 14-B of the Taft-Hartley Amendment, and notoriously conservative. The legislature whipped out the Farm Bureau bill, hardly paying any attention to the AFL-CIO threats of a nationwide boycott of all Arizona products."[18]

Simultaneously with passage of the bill, Governor Williams was leaving for a meeting in Washington. Before he left, he signed the measure.

"As I recall, Cesar, or one of his henchmen wanted to have a meeting with me before I signed the bill. I was slated to go to Washington. The office told them I was going out of town. I hadn't kept fully on top of this labor dispute. I signed it and went off and then the volcano erupted!

"When I got back I was, at least on this issue, a pariah in the state.

"There were numerous church denominations preaching sermons against me, including the Catholic and the Episcopal churches. The Episcopal Bishop of my own church hammered me. I went to other churches, and at one, the pastor said, 'Now let us all stand and say a prayer for Cesar Chavez!' Every day at the capitol, two nuns walked a picket line. Of course, the farmers loved me and so did the businessmen. But the wrath of the liberal community was unanimous. This precipitated the recall drive. They collected a large number of signatures."

In his book, Taylor wrote about a decision to send Chavez aide Jim Drake to Arizona for an evaluation of the situation.

"Drake said, 'We had a lot of debate whether or not to try to do away with the bill, or to pick on all of the legislators who voted for the bill, or narrow the attack by taking just one political hostage and making him an example. So we decided to go after the governor, to recall him because he had been so bad. He had refused to see Cesar; he signed the bill without reading it. He was a very good symbol....' "[19]

Drawing upon a tactic he had used in California a few years earlier, Chavez began a fast in Phoenix on May 30, 1972, the day the bill was signed into law.

Drake said, "The fast was undertaken because Cesar wanted to change the system; he wanted to get people over their fears of organizing, so they would be willing to fight for the union, and he figured the best way to do that was to expend himself. We never lost sight of the fact that we did not want a new governor, but that we wanted to organize the people and in the process send a clear message to all politicians that they had to be responsive to the people, to the workers."[20]

Hundreds of farm workers from California came to Phoenix in support of Chavez. Stories of the event were carried nationally. An article in *The Arizona Republic* the day after the governor signed the bill headlined—"BLACKS URGED TO SUPPORT CHAVEZ".

The story said, "Mrs. Martin Luther King last night urged Arizona blacks to unite behind the fight by the United Farm Workers Union to repeal 'an unjust law' against farm laborers and to recall Governor Williams. Comparing the farm workers struggle to efforts of her late husband against 'oppressive laws' in the South during the 1960's, Mrs. Coretta King told a reporter following a Roman Catholic Mass in the Santa Rita Community Center that blacks have a 'moral obligation' to join 'the struggle' for the governor's recall."[21]

Chavez was hospitalized for close observation the following day. He ended his fast 23 days later.

A year later, almost to the day, petitions bearing more than 175,000 signatures were presented to the Secretary of State in Phoenix. If all were valid, the total was 67,000 more than needed to force a recall vote the following November.

Governor Williams remembers, "The Secretary of State found some bogus signatures and the recall was thrown out. Later, I wished I'd just let them go ahead with it. I'd have won. As it is, there has always been a cloud of suspicion my administration knocked out the recall petitions."

Stephen C. Shadegg, friend and colleague of Williams, wrote this had been a "very difficult period for the governor emotionally, physically and financially. For seven years he had devoted all his energies and talents to improving conditions for all the citizens of Arizona. Though the recall was defeated, this had been a very trying time."[22]

THE TRUNK MURDERESS!

It was Friday, October 23, 1931. 26 year old Winnie Ruth Judd, a medical secretary at the Grunow Memorial Clinic in Phoenix, sat at a table in a Los Angeles restaurant, laughing and joking with the others in her party. With her—her husband Dr. William C. Judd and her brother B. J. McKinnell. Also in the group, Maricopa County Attorney Lloyd Andrews, his deputy Harry Johnson and the chief of detectives for the Los Angeles Police Department, Joe Taylor, along with three of his men.

Less than 3 hours earlier, Winnie Ruth Judd surrendered to authorities and admitted killing two women in a duplex apartment on North 2nd Street in Phoenix.[23]

The slayings, and their grisly aftermath, made headlines throughout the United States.

Mrs. Judd was accused of shooting to death her friends, 32--year-old Agnes Anne LeRoi—an X-ray technician at the Grunow Clinic, and 24-year-old school teacher Hedvig Samuelson, then stuffing their bodies into two trunks for shipment by train to Los Angeles.

The victims were killed Friday evening, October 16, 1931. Samuelson's body had been dismembered. The trunks containing the two bodies were moved from the murder scene to Mrs. Judd's Brill Street apartment in Phoenix. There, they remained for about a day and a half. On the 18th, they were taken to Union Station in Phoenix to be loaded on the evening train for Los Angeles.

(Just four years earlier, young Jack Williams had been working on the same platform loading freight on trains headed out of Phoenix.)

The case would take on the dimensions of legend through the next 40 years.

Winnie Ruth Judd's Phoenix, a small town of under 50 thousand residents at the time of the killings, had not really begun to rise.

Dusty roads outnumbered paved ones.

Everyone knew everybody.

Power brokers knew where all the political and social ghosts were hidden. Back-scratching was the norm. Eyes winked routinely.

Judd was never tried in the death of Samuelson. Her trial for the murder of Agnes Anne LeRoi began on January 25, 1932. When it was over, she stood convicted. One month later she was sentenced to hang.

The date for her execution was to be April 28, 1933. Three days before the noose would have been tied around her neck, a Pinal County jury ruled she was insane. She was immediately transferred to the Arizona State Hospital in Phoenix.[24]

Williams recalls an additional twist bearing on his relationship to the Judd case! "Earl Nielsen at KOY decided to have her trial dramatized so we hired Jack Stewart, later of the Camelback Inn, for $1.00 a day to go to the trial and report it. He wrote the dramatization. I selected the actors hired to take the roles of trial participants. We broadcast these dramas each evening. It was a sort of sensational thing to do at the time."

The death sentence was commuted to life in prison in 1952 by Governor Howard Pyle.

Throughout her entire case there would never be a formal sanity hearing for Mrs. Judd.

Her incarceration in the state's mental hospital would become a perfunctory exercise through the years, first as authorities wrestled with what to do with her case, then as interest in it fell victim to the passage of time. The only element of her case to hold the attention of anyone as the years dragged on, was her repeated escapes from the hospital and the embarrassment caused the state by them. So adept was she at walking out of the place she became almost a folk-hero figure.

A reporter interviewing Mrs. Judd in 1990 wrote, "Winnie Ruth Judd still has the key to the front door of Arizona State Hospital. She giggles as she displays her precious, long-kept secret. It's such an ordinary key to have caused so much commotion; not much bigger than a common house key, the numbers 634 stamped on one side. It was her most sacred possession fifty years ago when she first used it; it's her most treasured keepsake today. It's retired now to a lacquered box she keeps next to her bed."[25]

Between October 1939 when she first escaped, and October of 1962 when she last got away, Judd fled seven times.

Her sixth escape, on Thanksgiving night 1952, lasted just two days.

The night she was returned to the state hospital she told a newspaper reporter, "I want to get out. I want a sanity hearing. There's nothing wrong with me. I had a fight, but I didn't kill anyone in the commission of a crime."

Mrs. Judd insisted she was sane and, if given a sanity hearing, could prove it. She denied charges by Dr. M. W. Conway, Superintendent of the Arizona State Hospital she was dangerous and a trouble maker.

"I don't fight at the hospital. I don't quarrel with the other patients or the attendants. They've helped me escape. Nurses have hidden me on the grounds until I could get away. Attendants have hidden me in their homes....would they do this if I were dangerous?"[26]

Ruth Judd was 56 years old when she escaped for the last time in 1962. She remained free for about 7 years, living in suburban San Francisco under an assumed name and background. In June 1969, authorities discovered who she was.

Arizona wanted her back. Extradition proceedings were initiated. Nationally known defense attorney Melvin Belli of San Francisco was retained by her friends in the Bay Area to fight off Arizona's desire. The legal actions delayed for more than 60 days, her return to the state. But on Monday afternoon, August 18, 1969, Ruth Judd was brought to Phoenix by Maricopa County Sheriff's Deputy Ralph McMillen.

Her Phoenix attorney Larry Debus immediately moved to have her remanded to the state prison rather than having her returned to the state hospital.

"The only way to get her a pardon was go get her out of the state hospital and put her in prison," Debus said.[27]

From the beginning, there had always been questions. Had she actually committed the murders herself? Was she merely an accomplice of the actual killer? Had she acted in self-defense...which was her initial claim upon surrendering to Los Angeles authorities? Those and other questions about the case were never resolved, but weighing heavily against her claim of self-defense was the ghastly manner in which the victims' bodies were handled.

On October 27, 1969, the Arizona Board of Pardons and Paroles convened a hearing for commutation of sentence for Winnie Ruth Judd. It was denied in a 2-1 decision.

Attorneys Debus and Belli were shocked.

Belli said "...I think the board was born too late. They should have been born at the time of the Spanish Inquisition and the Star Chamber period." He went on "...two of those board members must be sick. There is something very sinister in this ...either someone or something is being protected."

Addressing remarks to the governor, he wondered how Williams could continue to let them serve on the board, adding, "I am utterly and completely furious about this. It is one of the blackest marks on your state."

Following up in a letter to the governor, Belli said, "I'd like to borrow your whole Parole Board for my next Halloween party."[28]

Not until February 16, 1971, one month after Jack Williams began his third term in office, was another commutation hearing held.

This time the board voted 2-1 recommending commutation of sentence. But it would be left up to the governor to decide if commutation would be for time served, or perhaps for a specific length of time...such as 20 or 30 years to life.

Williams was attending a National Governors Conference in Washington and made no immediate comment on the board's recommendation. When he returned he said the decision would be a difficult one and he would not be hurried into making it.

"I debated what to do. She had been punished a great deal and there was a lot of pressure to let her go. In fact, while making a speech before some university students, a big banner was unfurled by a group sitting in the front row reading...'Free Winnie Ruth Judd'.

"I decided to put her back in prison, one year for every three years she had been gone. She served her time."

Disposition of the Judd case had been the subject of much debate in the state's legal arenas following her return from California. One of the key issues with parole board members, and others, was that Mrs. Judd under no circumstances should benefit financially from her story.

The days following the board recommendation grew into weeks...then months...still no decision.

Newspaper headlines through the spring and summer told the story. "Ruling Awaited From Governor On Judd Case"; "Williams Bides Time On Mrs. Judd Decision"; "Judd Decision Snagged".

Fall came.

Then, as Governor Williams prepared for a vacation in Spain, the decision was announced.

The Arizona Republic reported in its October 27, 1971 edition, "Governor Williams, last night paved the way for the parole of Winnie Ruth Judd, 66, by commuting the life sentence of the convicted trunk murderess of the 1930s." The report continued, "... in lieu of the life sentence her minimum sentence shall reduce to time served and her maximum sentence shall remain life imprisonment. Robert Macon, special assistant to the governor, quoted Williams as saying the action did not mean immediate release for Mrs. Judd. Macon said the governor's commutation decree would go to the Board of Pardons and Paroles, which has the final authority in determining whether she will be paroled."[29]

A hearing by the board was set for one month and two days later.

Three days before Christmas 1971, Judd was released on parole early in the morning, and driven to California by friends.

Another governor ten years later would sign the final papers releasing forever Arizona's 50 year hold on Winnie Ruth Judd.

A MARXIST AMONG US

In April 1968, Dr. Martin Luther King, Jr. was gunned down as he stood on a motel balcony in Memphis.

Late in the evening of June 5, 1968, in a kitchen hallway at a Los Angeles hotel, Sen. Robert F. Kennedy was shot moments after acknowledging victory in the California presidential primary. Kennedy died of his wounds the next day.

By summer of 1968, the number of U.S. forces in Vietnam approached 500,000. At year's end 30,000 Americans had died there. Protest demonstrations against the war, race riots in major cities in the country, turbulent and activist times were these in the United States as Jack Williams won re-election to his second term as governor of Arizona.

At Arizona State University in Tempe, most students were going about the normal pursuits of college life as defined by the sales pitch wording of the ASU Catalog; some were in pursuit of individual agendas. There were anti-Vietnam war rallies, demonstrations, protests, all of it. At the University of Arizona in Tucson, similar activities were occurring.

Many university professors were also sounding off on the issues in public and private forums on both campuses.

One of these, Dr. Morris J. Starsky, an associate professor of philosophy in his mid-30's, was creating the most controversy. Since his arrival at ASU in 1964, Dr. Starsky had been a burr under the saddle of the basically conservative political establishment in Arizona. He was affiliated for a while with Students for a Democratic Society and headed the Anti-war Phoenix Committee on Vietnam.

A self-avowed communist of the Marxist-Leninist tradition, Starsky engaged in often vituperative speech when provided a forum. By the end of the decade, he had rankled almost all levels of the establishment from the Arizona Board of Regents (the controlling body of the state's three universities) to the state legislature. He had engaged in anti-war demonstrations and rallies, delivered Socialist themed speeches and frequently thumbed his nose at the traditional institutions of a democratic society.

In November of 1968, Starsky was prominent among a

group of nearly 300 students and others who occupied the administration building at ASU in protest over a university contract with a linen and towel supplier. A year and a half later an action of the Board of Regents ended his stay at ASU.

Believe it or not, given the language employed routinely today by millions of Americans, Dr. Starsky was even taken to task in newspaper editorials in Phoenix over his penchant for obscenity in both his classroom dissertations and in public utterances. One example, he was convicted in a Tempe, Arizona Justice of the Peace Court of using loud, offensive and obscene language when denied permission to put up signs on the doors of Grady Gammage Auditorium at ASU.

In an editorial titled "Intellectual Dross", *The Phoenix Gazette* said following the conviction: "When Starsky disputed obscenity of the words, he said that he used them regularly while teaching at the university, and said he would not object to their being used to a young child."

The editorial concluded: "Outside the courtroom the question isn't so much whether Starsky's words were technically obscene as it is whether a man so hard up for the means properly to express himself can be a good teacher."[30]

Through months of legal wrangling, the conviction was overturned by another court.

But cursing was hardly the core cause for the turmoil swirling around Starsky. The outspoken professor, if not prudent, was bold.

In speech after speech, interview after interview, Starsky's position on his Socialist beliefs was never hidden.

He was quoted in a newspaper concerning capitalism, "Getting rid of it has to be our highest priority." The article continued, "He makes no bones about his dislike for capitalism, and thinks strongly that the system must and will fall in favor of a brand of socialism. In order to accomplish the changeover, Dr. Starsky says, there will have to be a revolution, a violent one like those in Russia, France and America."[31]

Political pressure began to mount on the Arizona Board of Regents to do something about Starsky.

Some lawmakers involved with appropriations were hinting if Starsky wasn't reined in, disciplined, the Regents' own budget might be held hostage. The threat drew editorial comment warning against linking Starsky's status with funding the Regents budget. One Republican lawmaker even suggested the entire board be forced to resign and a new more responsible one be appointed by the governor to replace it.

In January of 1970, Starsky dismissed a class in order to free time for him to attend an anti-war rally at the University of Arizona. The action and subsequent furor in the community, again brought discussion in the meetings of the Board of Regents. The talk centered more and more on dismissal and less and less on merely reining in the professor.

An editorial in *The Arizona Republic*, titled "Is He Putting Us On?" pointed out Starsky's arrogance. "Prof. Morris Starsky says the State Board of Regents have no right to discuss his activities at Arizona State University. Specifically, he says, it was none of the regents' business when he went to Tucson to take part in a student demonstration instead of teaching a class at Tempe."

The editorial quotes Starsky..."I contend that a discussion of my position as a professor is illegitimate and a clear violation of both my fundamental civil liberties and the integrity of the university." Starsky's comments quoted in the newspaper were included in a letter from him to the president of the Board of Regents.[32]

Governor Williams, by office a member of the Board of Regents, was receiving hundreds of calls supporting and opposing Starsky.

An ASU faculty committee was asked to determine if dismissal proceedings against Starsky should be initiated. The committee found no cause.

A member of the committee, sociology professor Dr. Leonard Gordon said, "Mr. Starsky was a stimulant. He had received permission from his department chairman to go to the U of A, and his students testified he had not carried propaganda into the classroom. In a large, major research university, you are going to have some faculty who have different views, and if you are really going to develop students, you need different views.

"As long as a teacher doesn't propagandize and the grades don't depend on the students agreeing with the teacher's views, it is good for the academic environment."[33]

In the wake of the faculty committee's "no cause" decision, the Board of Regents ordered university president H. K. Newburn to draw up formal charges. Testimony before ASU's Committee on Academic Freedom and Tenure began in the College of Law building on March 24, 1970, and ended about six weeks later. The testimony was contained in seven volumes totalling 1178 pages of typed transcript. The Committee on Academic Freedom and Tenure also refused to recommend dismissal.

Starsky was becoming more involved in demonstrations, on and off the ASU campus. He even led a group of protesters in a march on the home of Senator Barry Goldwater.

The national agony over Vietnam continued unabated. Four students were killed by national guardsmen at Kent State University in Ohio during a protest against the war on May 4, 1970.

On Wednesday, June 10, 1970, at its regular meeting, the Regents voted 8-0 to terminate Starsky's employment at Arizona State University upon expiration of his contract. In addition, he would agree to a leave of absence for the time left on his contract.

Part of the statement read at the meeting included the following: "The Board specifically finds that Dr. Starsky, by his own testimony, would not consider himself bound in the future to obey or enforce the rules and regulations of the University and this board."[34]

Williams remembers, "I flew back from a governor's conference in Utah for the meeting. Our attorney said, 'I warn you against taking this action. The legal effects will be that it will go on from court to court and year after year.'

"I could see the spines of the Regents beginning to melt. So, I said to them, 'I don't care what the costs will be. I don't think we should condone the University's employment of a man of this character to teach our young people.' The spines stiffened and they affirmed the ouster of Starsky.

"The prophecy was true. He brought suit after suit against us. I paid the attorney bills personally for most of the board. It went on year after year. And I'll admit if I had known I precipitated so much trouble, I might have caved in. But you never win by giving up to evil and this guy was a troublemaker in those days. It was a painful experience.

"I still have the testimony where Starsky, answering a question about whether he felt bound by the rules of the University, replied, 'No!'

"In fact, I used that as the most compelling argument with the regents when they upheld the dismissal.

"There is a fine point here. Professors have tenure and protection. They are supposed to be safe when they advocate radical ideas. The freedom of the university is at stake. Of concern to me is how far this should go. I don't know the parameters, but I do believe Starsky breached them. Anyway, it was a rough time and I think it turned out right."

Starsky's dismissal led to a seven year censure against ASU by the American Association of University Professors. It's goal—to discourage professors from seeking employment there. The censure was lifted in 1981 after the university agreed to pay Starsky $25,000 in back pay.

Morris Starsky never obtained a full-time teaching position at another university. He died in Cincinnati, Ohio, January 20, 1989, at the age of 55. In an obituary following, his widow Lorraine, said, "He was committed to his beliefs to the very end of his life. He never thought the price he paid was too high for the statement he made about freedom of speech in this country."[35]

Dr. Thomas Hoult a fellow professor and contemporary of Dr. Starsky's at ASU, wrote a scathing indictment of Arizona, and Governor Williams, two years after Starsky's ouster.

"In Arizona, in 1970, there occurred a series of events that thoughtful Americans will see as a 'sign'. These events constitute a warning to the nation: Beware of marching too far to the ideological right.

"Considered superficially, the events referred to involved nothing more than the firing of Dr. Morris Starsky from his job as an Arizona State University professor.

"...That it is an advanced symptom is clearly suggested by some of the associated happenings. These included a hearing that many felt was strongly reminiscent of the political trials held in totalitarian societies."

Dr. Hoult's contempt for the conservative leadership in Arizona generally, and Governor Williams specifically, in the early 1970's, is reflected in additional passages from his book.

"The state's voters have elected the governor...three times in succession even though (or perhaps because) he seems to favor simplistic analyses of complex phenomena...Governor Williams' statements suggest he functions in terms of a philosophy made up of more or less equal proportions of anti-intellectualism, credulous conservatism, and arbitrary elitism. It is apparently this philosophy which has led the governor to engage in some actions and make some appointments that, from an egalitarian and/or educated point of view, are most unfortunate."[36]

Chapter Nine

Yours Sincerely

For more than three decades Jack Williams' radio program, *Yours Sincerely*, was a fixture on KOY at 8:45 weekday mornings. Thousands of Arizonans in Phoenix and wherever the Arizona Network extended, could listen to his commentaries, wonderful "first person" reports on his world travels, community happenings, epigrams and homespun anecdotes. Occasionally he would review books, movies and music. Sometimes the content was hard news, as his assignments would take him to venues as disparate as the Grand Canyon and the Brandenburg Gate. Frequently, Williams would share letters sent to him by listeners.

The volume of his written material is so extensive we cannot present it all. However, some selected scripts are being included.

His opening to the program became his signature.

"Top o' the morning to you neighbor. It's another beautiful morning in Arizona, leave us all enjoy it!"

Here's an example of a couple of epigrams culled from one of his scripts.

"Something to think about this morning...one of the hardest secrets for a man to keep is his opinion of himself. And I also liked this one: The coating of civilization is so thin that it often comes off with a little alcohol."

More of those slices of philosophy, taken from his scripts, will be included in this chapter.

The scripts are presented just as they were written for broadcast, with minor edits to facilitate your reading. Now, Jack Williams, host of *Yours Sincerely*. Enjoy!

ARIZONA—BIRTHPLACE OF THE MOTEL

(Air Date: November 29, 1955)

(Williams included this item from United Press International)

"It was back in 1913 that a man in Douglas, Arizona, bought a half dozen tiny miners' cottages, dolled them up and began renting them to passing motorists.

Thus was born the motor court, or motel to use its more modern name. It grew with the automobile itself. By 1922, there were around six hundred of these so-called tourist camps. Only 10 years later, the total was up to several thousand. And right now, there are nearly fifty thousand of them throughout the United States, grossing about three hundred million dollars a year.

California leads the motel parade with upwards of seventy five hundred, Florida has thirty five hundred...New York more than three thousand and Texas about twenty five hundred.

Some of the newer motels are really plush. There's one in Texas—naturally—with 200 air-conditioned rooms, including suites with wood-burning fireplaces. Others have swimming pools, fenced-in playground for youngsters and even serve breakfast in bed.

A good motor court is nothing but a good hotel—minus bellboys and doormen with outstretched palms. The American Automobile Association, which inspects about twenty thousand motor courts a year, says more and more hotel trained personnel are coming into the motel field, which is all to the good.

One of the difficulties of this mushrooming industry is that a lot of inexperienced people went into it expecting to make a fast buck with a minimum of work...and the casualty rate among such entrepreneurs has been devastating.

A well-run motel needs the owner on hand seven days a week. For this grind, he can expect an average net income of fourteen thousand dollars a year.

The motel has had a tremendous impact on the hotel business—and not a pleasant one, either. To fight this comparative newcomer, hotels actually are going in for some of the advantages of the motor court.

"In Washington for example, a large downtown hotel built a parking garage next door and installed a lobby right in the garage, so guests can register as soon as they drive up.

Meanwhile, the motels keep getting fancier—all of which has led one cynic to predict that eventually, the motor court will be more like a hotel and the hotel more like a motor court."

COMMUNITY SERVICE/WORK ETHIC

(Air Date: November 22, 1963)

(A Williams commentary)

"There is something strange in this world of ours today that has an Alice In Wonderland touch.

We noticed where the Pullman porters are going to try for a 40 hour week—and that a labor convention believes a 35 hour work week will be too long—and actually a 20 hour week is envisioned. Man works 4 hours a day.

Now, we know all the theories of our high rate of productivity, and also we know that in labor's eyes, the shorter week is a make work plan for those who have no jobs.

But in the laboring man's eyes it's merely the beginning of overtime. And a good worker is going to go into overtime, or will go to another job when he finishes his four hour stint. But, let's say that's debatable, or that stringent legislation will be invoked to control the worker.

The perfectly amazing thing is most of the people I associate with put in not 4 hours a day...not 8 hours a day...but ten, twelve, fourteen hours a day.

Through the exigencies of being somewhat of a 'do-gooder' ourselves, and being exposed to a number of community projects, we are thrown with an executive group. These are the bosses and the professional men. Now honestly, it seems to me in our world we have reversed things—the working man who used to labor from dawn 'til dusk—quits at five and goes home and is off Saturdays and Sundays—and really has much better hours than the entrepreneur who (to quote Marx) has 'enslaved him'.

Oh, I know there's a certain group who play gin at the club, golf frequently, and trip here and there. But these are the spectacular exceptions.

This broadcast today is not in the nature of a jeremiad. It is, I hope, an objective view of a situation in our society at this particular time.

Last night at a community council meeting I sat next to Elmer Theis who is, depending upon the situation and the person reporting, a labor boss...or a labor leader.

"Suffice to say he is one of the top leaders in the labor movement in Phoenix—I presume Elmer goes to work at 8:00 or 8:30 a.m. Last night he ended his labors for labor and his community at 9:30 p.m. Perhaps he went on to another assignment, but that's at least 13 hours.

I have known and do respect many of our labor leaders in Arizona. We argue, they thump me around now and then...but that's the way the game is played. As men, I know how hard they work. I once said to Keene Brown, former Executive Secretary of AFL-CIO who put in 10 to 12 hours daily, 'Here you work like a slave to get shorter hours for your men—and I just saw a couple of your members sitting in a tavern down the street leisurely drinking beer and enjoying the free hours you've made possible.'

Last night I saw insurance executive George Bright at the end of at least a twelve hour day. Lawyers like Paul Roca, at least 12 hours—and he's been chairing a committee on a study of the USO which I'm sure has kept him far longer than 12 hours a day at work. Bill Reilly, utility magnate, who should have been home with his family, but who at great sacrifice is chairing not only the Human Relations Committee, but also is chairman of the State Board of Institutions.

I have an idea I'm not wording this very well. It is not my purpose to make a plea for sympathy for these people. They are competent. They are leaders. They are successful in their areas. And they are hard workers. There isn't a one of them who couldn't walk away from their responsibilities and still survive.

Yet, there they sat last night, discussing what? Well, the Holiday Bureau that will begin collecting the names of the unfortunates who exist in every society who might be forgotten at Christmas time. The 'luckless plots' Omar wrote about...the unfortunate ones who will receive at Christmas, an extra something. They discussed the Human Relations Commission, which is doing a yeoman's task in a controversial and delicate situation. They discussed the Phoenix Pupil Motivation Project, a study to determine what can be done to motivate pupils to continue their education. Important? Yes! And if successful, it could well solve our problems of delinquency and unemployment. The so-called inner city problems, and the relation of the multi-problem family. This is the family to which everything happens...unemployment, illness, delinquency and tragedy.

These executives chairing these committees deal with serious subjects, affecting our community. These people are accustomed to making decisions—and to making things happen.

No, it is not sympathy for these poor benighted executives and professional people, it's only an observation of a twist in our national structure that for the first time in history, apparently, gives the laboring man more leisure than the man who employs him.

And perhaps this isn't quite an accurate description. But the fact remains, somewhere down the line, the truth comes out that in certain types of work, time is the only raw material that makes the difference. And let me confess my prejudice in this matter. It is my belief that work is important, that work is necessary and that work has a therapeutic value that cannot be over estimated.

I am convinced within reason that leisure is the most difficult of man's possessions to handle. It is in leisure hours that neurosis have an opportunity to develop, that self-pity has a field day, that Satan appears.

Now, this is my prejudice. It is distinctly a Western idea. And it is part of the economic foundation of our country. We are (or have been) a hard work oriented society. Not all societies are thus constituted, and we have changed in the last twenty or thirty years. At one time, any man who loafed was considered somewhat an object of scorn. Recreation was not glorified. It was the man who worked who counted.

Perhaps it wasn't a sound philosophy, but it produced a lot of material things—and also the leisure that plagues us today.

Somehow into our society has crept or is beginning to creep an aversion to work. The man who works is looked down upon...or the work he does is looked down upon. It started with Edwin Markham's 'Man With The Hoe'—the picture and the poem—I forget who painted the picture, and the Tale Of The Shirt. I have suddenly wondered what right had Markham to question the dumb, dull, brutish visage of the man with the hoe?

"What callous indifference to man's soul and what snobbishness he possessed. How did he know but what beneath his beetling brow, the man with the hoe thrilled to the touch of warm, loamy soil, and the flash of dawn across the crescent skies, and the whisper of spring in the evening wind. Not too long ago I visited briefly with an 80 year old pioneer of our valley, who has a ranch east of Mesa.

'What you been doing?' I asked. 'Oh, I've been out hoeing the ditches.'

He liked to hoe, he made hoeing a part of life. He wasn't crazy. He was remarkably well preserved, in good health, but he knew that work has a therapy that beats a rocking chair or an invalid's couch. He knew that an active life was one of effort and achievement."

SOUTH PACIFIC

(Air Date: November 11, 1955)

"Top o' the morning to you neighbors. Something to think about this morning: There are more home permanents these days than permanent homes. And I also liked this one: One way to keep your head above water is to keep out of expensive dives.

Well, it's another beautiful morning in Arizona, leave us all enjoy it.

It didn't dawn on Williams last night until after we had entered the West Phoenix High Auditorium and sat down and looked around that I was attending a first night.

Rather vaguely, I knew Miss Vera, my bride of some 12 summers and 13 winters or vice versa, had tickets to *South Pacific* and she wanted to go. She is the music lover in the Williams family, and in her behalf the two boys (sons Ric and Mic) dutifully practice finger exercises on the piano each week and the young lady (daughter Nikki) goes to dancing class.

It was a gala crowd into which I plunged. The entire Paradise Valley Country Club set sat in front of me. Or sat set in front...(I like it better that way).

The beautiful West High auditorium was packed. I saw Anson B. Cutts, the critic. Also Miss Bobby Johnson of the *Gazette*. I wondered what Mr. Cutts would say this morning.

Let me just say that a guy by the name of John Frazee burst upon the Phoenix audience last night in *South Pacific* and gave a rendition (in the role of Frenchman Emile DeBecque) that had everybody talking. If complications of getting the cast on the stage and the flowers on the stage and the curtain back and forth at the end hadn't gotten out of hand, I think Mr. Frazee would have been given a standing ovation. He never showed up alone though.

I thought Bob Pollard and Ben Roush were especially well cast. Miriam Root was splendid as Bloody Mary. My only criticism is the costume department could make her more unattractive. I think the beetle nut juice should stain her lips a little more, and they ought to black out her front teeth. She still looks too human, and nice. But she played the part to perfection. The guy that stole the show for my money was Billis—Luther Billis—er, I mean Jack Lang. I have a hunch Lang played himself to some extent. He was a typical caricature of the self-sufficient Sea Bee's on a lonely island.

Let me say this was real theater, this production by the Phoenix Civic Opera. Wonderful stage settings and fast scene shifts, terrific lighting, good use of scrim. The orchestra was good...oh so very good.

Being a native, I can only marvel at a community like ours that is lifting itself by its own bootstraps, so to speak, into the sun. On every side you can see the growth of our community; economically, culturally, physically. And perhaps if we all work together we can work some improvement in the only area where we still lag behind the rest of the nation—health wise. Our record is bad there. But why interject a note of anything but exultation as a result of last night's experience."

CONFIRMATION

(Air Date: December 10, 1955)

"Top o' the morning to you neighbors. Something to think about this morning: No man can make good during working hours who does wrong after working hours. It's another beautiful morning in Arizona. Leave us all enjoy it. Monday morning chuckle. The twins, five years old had knelt for bedtime prayers. Little Clara prayed first, concluding: 'Amen, good night, God. And now stay tuned for Clarence!'

Williams is easily affected by sentimental things. I seem not far ever from a lump in the throat and tears in the eyes. Beautiful music, a sad ending to a story, a picture, a thought...will touch off some responsive part of the human mechanism that has that effect on me.

Sunday morning at our church, we had what is called Confirmation. The youngsters joined the church by confirming the things either they or their sponsors had promised for them at baptism. It is an ancient and significant ceremony. Almost every race and culture has such affairs. And in our modern world with all of the scientific gadgets and the rush and the bustle, it was touching for me to see the candles, and the ceremony, and the girls with their white veils, and the boys with their hair combed and their freckles shined up.

I watched as the girls, aged 12 and 13, walked down the aisle toward the alter...looking like little pilgrims which in fact they were. Each of them made a curtsy, then turned into a pew. The boys, more awkward and self-conscious, followed and took their places as well.

Back through the ages of our Western culture and into the old Judean past went the threads of yesterday's ceremony. For as long as man has had a concept of something to worship he has made a ceremony of bringing his children to the temple and presenting them at the alter.

Old phrases, softened and mellowed with time, echoed through the cathedral and fell like a caressing benediction on the bowed heads of the youngsters. Phrases their fathers and their father's fathers had heard in one form or another...some of them penned as early as the epistles of St. Paul, two thousand years ago. Others, coming out of the mists of vast antiquity from the thundering slopes of Mt. Sinai, or the shores of the Red Sea.

I thought of the normal progression; up an aisle in a church, baptism, confirmation, communion, marriage and finally the last rites. The normal progression of youth and age and mankind. The closer you come to normalcy, the happier you are; the traditional things that form a foundation for any society, the things fathers have savored and found good and passed along to their sons. The hardships that are normal that other people have suffered, are not as difficult to accept as the weird new things that happen in an unconventional society.

This of course, is my philosophy—perhaps not yours. And since this morning I am talking about a traditional experience, it is very close and real to me. If there is a way of happiness for mankind, and there is no guarantee of it on earth, it would come, I think through the practice of the 'golden mean'—moderation. Yet there are those restless souls who preach extremes—the frenetic geniuses who live in garrets or on the Left Bank and who write eccentric poetry, or paint incomprehensible pictures. Or sculpt agonized forms. They lend their mark to the future, but are seldom if ever happy with the present.

So, I looked at the little girls and the little boys, conscious of their new maturity, and thought of all the things they must face in the years ahead. The fearsome moments of lonely adolescence when the strange emotions that beset them, come for the first time and have no answer from the past. The feeling of futility and the strange, sad sweetness of an unrequited romance. The dances and the parties. The temptations and the prayers. And the hurt that will come and the triumphs. And I hoped that part of the normalcy that could level out the bumps would come to them through the comforting religion they were exposed to.

And I thought of the great fellowship of Christians they joined, followers of Christ, so called first at Antioch.

And I hoped the confusion of our modern world, which has proposed more questions than it has answered actually, would resolve itself better for them than for the last two generations. Because, you see, I think that while we have won the world with our civilizations, we are in danger of losing our souls. I think we are the smartest civilization yet, and the most unhappy.

The economic exploitation of the masses has disappeared to a degree in the United States that would have sounded fantastic in Marx' time. The working classes have an increasing share in the national wealth and it is a perfectly valid assumption that, provided no major catastrophe occurs, there will be in about one or two generations, no marked poverty in the United States. The worker through his unions, has become a social partner of management. He cannot be ordered around, fired, abused, as he was even thirty years ago. As far as submission to irrational authority goes, the picture has changed drastically since the nineteenth century.

Children are no longer afraid of their parents. They are for the most part, 'companions' and if anybody feels slightly uneasy, it is not the child, but the parents who fear not being up to date.

Looked upon from the standards of the nineteenth century, we have achieved almost everything which would have seemed necessary for a happier society. But, in the country which is the most democratic, peaceful and prosperous, there is evidence of the most severe symptoms of mental disturbances. This type of civilization has the highest rate of insanity, suicides and alcoholism. My statistics come from the World Health Organization reports from Geneva.

It was during the first part of this 20th century that we left the church if you will remember. Now, we are returning to it, I hope. As the paradox goes, religion inspires frugality—frugality begets wealth—and wealth makes a man indifferent to religion. John Wesley said that back in the 18th century.

Perhaps one of the reasons I felt so impressed at yesterday's confirmation ceremony, was seeing again the procession of new members going down the aisle to join the church...returning to a normalcy that might promise more happiness or at least more serenity and peace of mind."

A LETTER TO FUTURE AMERICANS

(Air Date: October 14, 1963)

(This letter was included in the program on the above date.)

By Jim Griffith, Jr., Editor, *Lusk* (Wyo.) *Herald*

"To My Great-Great-Grandchildren:

Inasmuch as we shall never meet, I want to leave you this note of appreciation.

You see, it was during my lifetime that the leaders of the United States decided to spend some of the tax money that your great grandparents, grandparents, parents and you, and most likely your descendants, would have to pay.

Thank you for your generosity.

Our practice of deficit financing was started during a financial depression and was necessary. It was necessary to continue the practice through a great war, called World War II. Following World War II, the United States had a period of long prosperity, but we had grown accustomed to spending more tax money than we liked to pay. Rather than paying off what we had borrowed, we decided to let you do it.

I hope you won't hate the memory of my generation. Mostly, they were darn fine people. They would have liked to leave you the same rich, debt-free heritage that they received, but in the name of progress we had to get money from someone. We took it from you. Thanks.

With appreciation,

Great-Great-Grandpa Jim"

THE HOME CLINIC
(Air Date: June 8, 1950)

"There is probably no average family better equipped, theoretically, for sudden emergencies of a medical or home nursing type than the Williams family. My helpmate...or is it helpmeet...took all the Red Cross home nursing courses during the war that were offered. We also just happen to have a large book at home which is a family physician. I can't think of the name of it; but one purchases such a tome for emergencies in order to identify certain types of crises that arise in the family. When first we acquired the book some years ago, I noticed, with some misgivings, the illustrations were not of the most modern type to put it mildly. The men are shown in high, stiff collars and wearing watch chains across their vest fronts; the women are attired in small-waisted outfits, draped ungracefully to their ankles, a style out of the era of the 1900's I believe.

The book did go into explicit detail on symptoms of various kinds. It was vague about remedies, but the symptoms were appallingly practical. Or so it seemed. Anyway, with such a background, we felt reasonably secure against the frailties of the flesh out at our house.

Of course, during matters of mild emergencies, the good wife got so excited she couldn't remember which of the Red Cross home nursing instructions to apply; and we all compromised on the hand wringing exercise. When Ric fell on the furnace, we wrung our hands vigorously until a nearby neighbor came in and applied butter to the wound, under the mistaken impression that any grease was a good preventative for a burn. Let me digress here for a moment. Butter is not good for burns. Butter has salt in it. Salt in a wound is not recommended, even by your worst enemy. Anyway, after this experience, and when Ric returned from the doctor's office, we felt that the home nursing course was fine, but we needed a little practical experience in applying the measures.

Usually we compromised by rushing the injured member to the nearest doctor or hospital.

In the early days of our family, the catastrophes consisted of injuries and since the children could not describe symptoms, we did not make full use of the medical book.

Lately, we have turned with a great deal of interest to the various sections of the book dealing with the more familiar childhood diseases. A complaint of a sore throat brings out the book. Then follows a period of intense reading, and questioning. Where does it hurt? Can you swallow? Which ear has the buzzing in it? This latter complaint went on at some length, and even included a certain amount of treatment, until we found out that the buzzing in the ear was a mosquito in the room. Our five-year-old Mic, had difficulty differentiating between the buzz or whine of a mosquito NEAR his ear and a buzz IN his ear.

Finally, about three weeks ago, we put the medical book to the supreme test. Our eldest, who is a bit of a hypochondriac anyway, has a vivid and satisfying method of describing symptoms. We traced each of the aches and pains and problems and although for a while were off on a wrong section and almost concluded that the lad was coming down with either Burger's disease or a little-known and deadly South African cramp, we at last got on the track and diagnosed his case triumphantly as measles!

A few hours later when the good doctor arrived, and the lad had blossomed out with what we felt vaguely might be a violent case of hives, we learned he had a full blown case of chicken pox.

And despite the book saying chicken pox is a mild children's complaint, I am assuring you that the point of a pin would not go between the eruptions on the face and body of our eldest unmarried scion of the Williams family.

Little Mic could hardly wait the requisite two weeks so that he could get as many chicken pox as his older brother. And get them, he did! Next came his fourteen month old sister, whose button nose could hardly accommodate the number of chicken pox clustered there. Her mother's horror was exceeded only by the young lady's nonchalance about the matter. Mother knew that a scar on the nose would handicap the possibilities of the young lady in the matrimonial field a few years hence. So, mother started a king size worry about those pock marks on the tiny nose. Relays of watchers were established to prevent the little lady from scratching her nose. Night vigils sapped Mrs.

W.'s strength.

'Twas but a week ago that we brought out the big medical book again. Mrs. W. described her symptoms carefully, while I read with deep interest, the various sections that seemed to apply.

Finally I announced, 'YOU HAVE MUMPS!'

'But, I had mumps as a girl', Mrs. Williams interjected.

I replied authoritatively, 'All the symptoms are here, and it says sometimes you have them twice'.

Mrs. W. continued her protest, 'I just can't have mumps!'

'The book says it's mumps and you'll have to go to bed!'

In the morning, the doctor came. By then the "mumps" were really giving Mrs. Williams a time. Solemnly, we told the doctor what was wrong. He, upon casual, but professional inspection, dismissed the mumps diagnosis and proceeded to make arrangements to send Mrs. W. to the hospital with a good case of exhaustion and a strep infection. We secured the services of Mrs. Bonnie Frederickson to watch out for the three chicken pox cases at home and to take care of the distraught father-husband, Yours Truly!

Now, last night, I picked up that medical book again! And I started reading the section on housemaids knee!

You know, I have all the symptoms. But the thing is, all I did yesterday was mow the lawn!"

SHIP OF FOOLS

(Air Date: October 9, 1963)

"We have been devouring books, and failing to report on them with any degree of regularity. They still linger in my mind. One, written by the author of *Pale Horse, Pale Rider,* I understand will be made into a screen play. It is *Ship Of Fools,* which has received its first paperback printing of one million copies by New American Library under the Signet Label. The author, Katherine Anne Porter, has turned out a book that is uncomfortably real. And yet running through its macabre group of characters is an unrealism we attribute to life when it reaches its nadir.

How often have we heard truth is stranger than fiction. And how often have we later felt some unusual situation wasn't truly indicative of life.

So, with *Ship Of Fools,* a structure that fits some other dramatic situations such as the *Bridge of San Luis Rey.* Miss Porter concocts a deeply psychological tale of a German ship, with a motley passenger list, sailing back to Germany in 1935. *The New York Times* ranked it with the greatest novels of the past hundred years.

The reason, I'm sure, is that aboard the ship and confined to the limitations of the ship were the emotional catalysts that produced the Nazi mind, the Jewish purge, the frustrating, heart breaking, apparently impossible-of-solution human relations between various races and various mores and various psychological quirks.

The Jew in the book is no better than the German Nazi. The American girl as bad as the gypsy prostitute. The steerage passenger who threw himself overboard and lost his life saving a dog was the only bright character in the book.

It was almost as though you were reading about a carnal 'House of Horrors' or a mad house of impossible characters with a tenseness and a dramatic intensity that made it most upsetting to read.

Louis Auchincloss called it a vivid, beautifully written story bathed in intelligence and humor. Well, I could not find the humor, but it was certainly bathed in intelligence. It was a tragedy, or is a tragedy. And its characters, to me, all tragic, all frustrated fools, being carried to a destination that was inevitable as death.

Miss Porter gives you a lengthy cast of characters on her first page, then proceeds to develop each character as skillfully as any dramatist could ask.

Her shipboard scenes smell of steerage, spilled sour wine and musty quarters.

A thoroughly disturbing book and yet, a book that will help give perspective to the eternal relationship of human beings, one to another."

DAUGHTER—AS NURSE!

(Air Date: December 6, 1955)

"During a recent minor illness we made the most delightful acquaintanceship with a young lady, age six, who happens to be our daughter.

It is out of such things that memories are woven. And I am sure Miss Nikki, who for some time has owned a 'Nancy Nurse' outfit, will also keep a profound memory of this recent period that father spent in bed.

Up to now, a whole family of dolls have received the ministrations of our Nancy Nurse. Dutifully, they have had their temperatures taken, cold compresses placed on their heads, sips of water and pillow proppings.

For the initial periods of my malaise, my diminutive nurse, with honey-colored pigtails, spent her spare time inquiring diligently after our comfort. With a proprietary hand she smoothed the covers, brought innumerable glasses of water and small pieces of cotton, and answered the 'phone.

Later we took up the study of chess. But during the first periods...man could ask no more faithful attendant than six year old Miss Nikki in her nurses outfit.

Gone was the tomboy roughness that characterizes her relationship with the boys. And in its place, a tenderness that was as exquisitely feminine as it was proprietary. Somewhere out of the eternal mystery God has placed in womanhood, the essential mothering instinct stirred and came to life. Measured by only six short years, it was there. The tiny flickering beginnings of whatever inspired Nightingale or the nurse at Dien-Bien-Phu.

Sure, she had freckles on her nose, but she had love in heart and a strange compelling urge to help that brought her back to the bedside as a moth to a flame.

It so happened that the Thanksgiving Holiday and the Friday, Saturday and Sunday following, were school-less days. And so, our tiny nurse had ample time to practice her ministrations.

Sure, toward the end of the period, a new turtle who joined

our family, was added to the wide circle her tiny heart encompasses. And as the novelty of Daddy in bed wore off and the charm of a turtle in a new aquarium took over, father was more and more neglected.

But, I have my memories and she has hers. And if this time, I lose to a rather ungainly and awkward turtle, in time I shall lose again...to an ungainly and awkward youth who will finally absorb all her time. Then, as now, I shall hold firmly in my memories, the little girl that used to be...and thank the Holy Trinity for having had her once."

GOD IN SCHOOL
(Air Date: November 1, 1963)

"There's an interesting and somewhat upsetting trend in our country to remove God from the schools. Most of this activity is based on rulings from the Supreme Court, and in view of the position of the court, I can't agree with them, but I can't see how they can do anything else.

Certain clergymen have either applauded or accepted these rulings against prayers, etc., by the court. I am wondering what the same clergymen are going to do when the court rules the state has no right to make laws providing exemptions for church property.

I honestly don't see how the court, to be consistent, can help but rule in each instance, against God! I think what is happening is the court is ruling in favor of agnostics.

But I am not very smart in such things and lawyers have made a career of law and its interpretations and I shall not attempt to go very deeply into the subject, because it is involved. Suffice to say in my layman's opinion, if the court is to be consistent, it must ultimately rule against chaplains in the Army, In God We Trust on the coins, and probably rule out the last stanza of the *Star Spangled Banner*...and the Pledge of Allegiance.

Yet, in the beginning of our country, almost every great address or document had reference to God, to a divine providence, to the Great Ruler of the universe.

And after reading a great number of them the other night, I wondered what such men as those who prepared the great speeches and documents in and around 1775 and through the early 1800's would say at the calculated effort to do away with God. We tend to forget something I read about the other day...just as a circle has no beginning or end, so God inhabiteth eternity—He is without beginning of days or length of years.

...We all used to assume what our forefathers had in mind was to prevent the establishment of a state religion, an official religion of state, but actually the vast majority just took for granted that the (to them) all embracing Christian religion would be, in effect, the basic religion of this country. And there would be room, without persecution, for the tacit acceptance and acknowledgment of Judaism and any other religion, although actually they had little contact with Mohammedism despite the fact the Turks still occupied part of Europe while our founding fathers were framing our constitution and government."

SATCHMO

(Air Date: November 15, 1955)

"Top o' the morning to you neighbors. Something to think about this morning: When your knees are knocking, kneel on them. And I also liked this one: The only one who should place faith in a rabbit's foot is a rabbit. Well, it's another beautiful morning in Arizona. Leave us all enjoy it.

I have just finished reading a new Signet Book on the stands called 'Satchmo'—the riotous story of the one and only Louis 'Satchmo' Armstrong. A wonderfully alive and explosive auto-biography of the gravel voiced, golden horned jazz man, Armstrong, who grew up in back alley honky-tonks of New Orleans, fighting savagely for his existence.

I found something in the book the jazz lover will not, perhaps. I found a strange surprise for me in the fact that running deftly through the pages is a faith of a little colored boy in a system that would give him a chance—regardless of the way the deck would seem stacked against him. It's a sort of Horatio Alger story, only different, because Horatio Alger in this story started far lower than any of the original heroes. But, like a golden thread through the book, is Louis' tremendous energy and drive to work. I found the repetition of the names of the great horn blowers somewhat boring, and the constant reference to the great bands of that early era left me a little cold.

But such paragraphs as this made the reading worth while for me: 'Ever since I was a baby I have had great love for my grandmother. She spent the best of her days raising me and teaching me right from wrong. Whenever I did something she thought I ought to get a whipping for, she sent me out to get a switch from a big old China Ball tree in her yard.'

'You been a bad boy,' she would say. 'I am going to give you a good licking.'

'With tears in my eyes, I would go to the tree and return with the smallest switch I could find. Generally, she would laugh and let me off. However, when she was really angry she would give me a whipping for everything wrong I had done for weeks.'

Armstrong's words continue, 'In those days, of course, I did

not know a horn from a comb. I was going to church regularly
for both grandma and great grandmother were Christian women,
and between them they kept me in school, church and Sunday
School.'

Throughout the book, Satchmo tells of his jobs.

'As I grew older, I began to sell newspapers so as to help
make both ends meet.'

He also described his life at the Colored Waif's Home For
Boys.

'The waifs home was surely a clean place and we did all the
work ourselves. The first thing we did to a newcomer was to
make him take a shower and his head and body were carefully
examined to see that he didn't bring any vermin into the home.
Every day we had to line up for inspection. Anyone whose
clothes were not in proper condition was pulled out of line and
made to fix them himself. Once a week we were given a physic,
when we lined up in the morning and very few boys were sick.
The place was more like a health center or a boarding school
than a boys' jail. We played all kinds of sports and we turned
out some mighty fine baseball players, swimmers and musicians. All in all, I am proud of the days I spent at the Colored
Waif's Home For Boys.'

Incidentally, he also learned to play the trumpet there. But
what a philosophy. Everything that happened was for the best
with Louie. Never in the whole book does he sound like he knew
what self pity was.

While he played horn at night, he had all the ambition in the
world.

'I got another job driving a coal cart during the day. After
I finished work at four in the morning, I would run back home
and grab a couple of hours sleep. Then I would go to the C.A.
Andrews Coal Company at Ferret and Perdido Streets, two
blocks away from the honky-tonk. From seven in the morning
until five in the evening, I would haul hard coal at fifteen cents
per load. And I loved it. I was fifteen years old and felt like a
real man when I shoveled a ton of coal into my wagon. Being
young and small as I was, I could not make over five loads a day.
But I was not doing so bad. The seventy-five cents I made in the

day, plus the dollar and a quarter plus tips I made in the tonk, added up. In those days it was a good thing to have a steady job. Because there was always the chance that the cops might close the tonk down.'

There are other things in the book. It is not a good book for young to read because Louie was thrown with the worst riff raff of New Orleans. And grew up with them. But if you like the early history of jazz, you'll thrill to the stories of King Oliver and the great Dixieland bands of the turn of the century period. You'll march with the bands in funeral parades, a high point for musicians in those days, and you'll ride the tail gate with Louie himself.

You may be shocked if you read this book. But, read it with sympathy if you do. You'll find Satchmo in parades and at funerals, playing irresistibly and wildly on his hot trumpet in honky-tonks and brothels and on a Mississippi steam boat and with the jazz greats. He speaks frankly about the back o' town New Orleans slum where he was raised, of his vivacious ma and his long succession of step-fathers, of street brawls, waged with razors and bottles. But running throughout is the energy of a boy raised to tell the difference from right and wrong, and to take a physic every week for his health. A little boy who started out with the entire deck stacked against him, but never knew it; who played the horn and shoveled coal; who sold newspapers and worked on a milk route; a boy who was taught to be respectful and polite.

Jazz lovers will meet the members of the Superior Brass Band—Joe "King" Oliver, Freddy Keppard, Honore Dutrey, Johnny Dodds, Joe Howard, Fats Marable, Warren "Baby" Dodds and "Kid" Ory. But I've already told you the part I liked the best. And you may not like the book at all. Only it is for me, a profound testament to American Democracy."

TRAVELIN' MAN

(Air Date: October 18, 1963)

(Author's note: The following is extracted from a program Williams did concerning a flight he made from Luke Air Force Base west of Phoenix, to New Orleans. It is included in order to share with the reader of this biography, the skillful, magnificent word pictures this broadcaster painted for his listeners time and time again.)

"The...view of our valley from the sky is always interesting, because it is a checkerboard of greens and yellows and browns...laid out with geometric exactness.

The contrast of the wilderness of Superstition Mountains, the jewel like quality of the lakes that linger on a thread of river below, the tumultuous terrain of the canyon country, the great spread of Ponderosa forest below and then the bleak enchantment of New Mexico...followed by the utter desolation of the strip and the vastness of Texas...all flow beneath one's plane in an uninterrupted strip of unreality.

I can't remember any cities until someone said..there's Houston and sure enough I glanced down and saw big, sprawling Houston with its Buffalo Bayou and its cluster of great buildings, and most important of all, the winding ship canal that makes this inland Texas city one of the great sea ports of the world.

It seems to me someone once said Houston was built on a bayou area that never should have attracted a city, that it had everything wrong with it, to make it a big city. But with indomitable will...it simply dug a ditch to the gulf and plumbed the earth for oil and lifted itself by its own bootstraps into the major city of Texas. I could see the great freeways below, the complex of subdivisions, the parks, and then as we kept flying eastward, the San Jacinto Monument and the Battleship Texas, a tiny toy moored below, there on that green pasturage so far below us. Once the great Sam Houston soundly defeated Santa Ana, catching him by surprise.

I could see the Trinity River and thought back years ago to a catfish and hush puppy fry on its banks. Then we saw the Gulf with patches of afternoon fog, and Galveston with its sea wall, and later, Lake Charles, and the estuary where are buttoned up some of the tiny torpedo boats of World War Two in long lines of moored craft.

We flew along a narrow path because many portions of the Gulf today are barred to planes. They are areas like our gunnery range near Ajo. Only these gunnery ranges are out over the Gulf itself. And in many instances, missiles as well as bombs and bullets are used and it's no place for a friendly plane.

New Orleans looked big, too. And Lake Pontchartrain was another khaki colored sheet of water below, colored so by the late evening mist..."

GO HOME!

(Air Date: October 25, 1963)

(Williams included the following in his broadcast on the above date. It is from a Juvenile Court Judge in Denver, Colorado. Judge Phillip B. Gilliam said:)

"Always we hear the plaintiff cry of the teenager: 'What can we do?...where can we go?' The answer is go home!

Hang the storm windows, paint the woodwork. Rake the leaves, mow the lawn, shovel the walk. Wash the car, learn to cook, scrub the floors. Repair the sink, build a boat, get a job.

Help the minister, priest or rabbi, the Red Cross, the Salvation Army. Visit the sick, assist the poor, study your lessons. And then when you are through and not too tired—read a book.

Your parents do not owe you entertainment. Your city or village does not owe you recreational facilities. The world does not owe you a living...you owe the world something. You owe it your time and energy and your talents so that no one will be at war or in poverty or sick or lonely again.

In plain, simple words, grow up; quit being a crybaby. Get out of your dream world and develop a backbone, not a wishbone, and start acting like a man or a lady.

You're supposed to be mature enough to accept some of the responsibility your parents have carried for years. They have nursed, protected, helped, healed, appealed, begged, excused, tolerated and denied themselves needed comforts so that you could have every benefit. This they have done gladly, for you are their dearest treasure. But now, you have no right to expect them to bow to every whim and fancy just because selfish ego instead of common sense dominates your personality, thinking and requests.

In Heaven's name, grow up and go home!"

CHRISTMASTIME '55

(Air Date: December 23, 1955)

"Top o' the morning to you neighbors. Something to think about this morning: The weakest spot in every man is where he thinks himself to be the wisest. And I also liked this one: If you find nothing else to smile at, there is always yourself. Well, it's another beautiful morning in Arizona. Leave us all enjoy it.

There are a few vignettes I discovered the other evening downtown. Christmas carolers in an open top city bus parked in front of the court house at city hall, serenading the prisoners who thronged the north side of the "tanks" on the top floor of that edifice...what a bleak prospect, to be in jail on Christmas.

Patient smiles of the Salvation Army ladies and the hurrying crowds pushing past their Christmas kettles. The small boy who darted from his parent's company to thrust some change into the kettle. A radio announcer conducting a man on the street broadcast in Spanish in front of Walgreen's...an off-duty police officer in plain clothes watching for shoplifters in Penny's.

Civilian defense volunteers in blue uniforms directing traffic at main intersections. Tired Santa Claus mopping his brow. Bored men in company of their wives standing in lingerie departments. Bored wives standing with their husbands in hunting and camping departments.

The star atop the Professional Building and the tower atop the Westward Ho. The blind man with his white cane feeling his way through the crowds who pushed to listen to the Christmas carols.

The bars with their lonely figures nursing a drink as they slump on a bar stool. Phoenix—a few nights before Christmas."

(Air Date: December 26, 1955)

"Top o' the morning to you neighbors. Something to think about this morning: Santa enters through a hole in the chimney and leaves through a hole in father's pocket. And I also liked this one: A youngster is growing up when he finds out that the opinions of a department store Santa Claus, do not necessarily reflect those of his parents. Well, it's another beautiful morning in Arizona. Leave us all enjoy it.

How did Christmas day go for you? Well, I hope! Probably one of the most beautiful Christmas days ever seen anywhere!

At our house, we wanted to have a fire in the fireplace, but the only way to do it would have been to turn on the refrigeration in order to cool the place down enough to stand a fire. At the studio, here, we did have the refrigeration going, as the thermometer climbed past the 80 mark.

To the residents of the Valley of the Sun came the best Christmas present of all—a truly beautiful Christmas day!

Churches were reported crowded. I hope many returned thanks for the day and breathed a prayer for those who lived in neighboring states and who faced tragedy and calamity.

I have watched with interest the remarks of those who would criticize Christmas; the preacher who didn't like the way Bing Crosby sang Christmas carols; the individual who decried the commercialism of Christmas; the man who complained about Christmas cards and the woman who was upset because Christmas carols were sung on the streets of Phoenix.

Alfred North Whitehead in his book *Adventures Of Ideas,* points out in every civilization at its culmination, a certain amount of perfection is to be found. This culmination can maintain itself so long as fresh experimentation within the type is possible. When these minor variations are exhausted, staleness then sets in. Repetition produces a gradual lowering of vivid appreciation. Convention dominates. The last flicker of originality is exhibited by the survival of satire.

Satire does not necessarily imply a decadent society, though it flourishes upon the outworn features in the social system. It was characteristic at the close of the Silver age of Roman culture. Shortly after the deaths of the Younger Pliny and of Tacitus, the satirist Lucian was born.

Again, at the close of the Silver age of the Renaissance culture, during the 18th century, Voltaire and Edward Gibbon perfected satire in their various styles. Satire was natural to the age as it neared the American Revolution. The crash of the great World War I marked another end. But the close of that epoch was marked also, by the rise of satire again—Lytton

Strachey in England...Sinclair Lewis in the United States. Whitehead claims satire is the last flicker of originality in a passing epoch as it faces the onrush of staleness and boredom. Freshness has gone. Bitterness remains.

I don't know why this passage came to my mind concerning Christmas —except when I hear criticism of Christmas I can't help but thank God for Christmas. The one time when so many do such nice things. The thoughtful, wonderful things.

Christmas eve, I found Montague Machell all by himself playing Christmas carols on cello at the Valley of the Sun Rest Home. What a generous, nice thing to do. The city bus drivers donated their time to drive carolers around the city and to take crippled children places; and all of the folks who adopted a family for Christmas or who went out of their way to do something extra nice.

I deplore the approach of cynicism at Christmas. Regardless of how much commercialism there is, the fact remains Christmas is the one time when most people think of someone else. When almost the whole world takes time out to give—instead of get!

Even the Christmas cards bring memories of friends whom I have little thought of through the long months since last Christmas. The smiles and the quietness of the Holy Day. Thank God for Christmas!"

OUR CHILDREN

(Air Date: December 28, 1955)

"So many of the great reforms have turned out to be boomerangs when we carry them to reform.

Retirement at a certain age—is working pitiful hardships on a certain class of middle aged worker who now cannot get a job. Child labor laws have succeeded in making our late teen-age youths, drones on the market. The one-dollar minimum wage will mitigate against youth employment in many industries.

In the past 100 years this nation has accomplished many of the most visionary plans of the most extreme idealists. It is amazing the tremendous reforms that have come about in this nation. We have not gone all the way, but we have gone so much further than any other nation in recorded history that we stand as an example of reform for history to refer to. What we have not done yet, is to make much change in human nature.

Our social reforms are predicated upon the perfect man, without prejudice, malice, envy, selfishness, hate, deceit. Until we effect some major change in man himself, we are going to be disappointed with our net result. Despite the advantages we have brought forth in this nation—high wages, leisure time, enlightened labor leadership, child labor laws, a juvenile code, we are not a particularly happy nation.

Social thinkers feel the reforms will reform the man, that without want, man will cease to be selfish, that with more leisure time, man will think more, that with cradle to the grave security, the tensions that produce neurosis will be lessened.

I do not know. Many of the hardships we have eliminated have produced some of our greatest men. Out of poverty and ignorance have come some of our greatest minds and leadership. The man who loses his job has gone to another better suited to him, and made a great success. The youth who worked the longer hours and saved his money frugally, became the great philanthropist of history.

What we are arguing in our juvenile code, is not just an isolated matter. When you make over the world to suit yourself—do you change the men and women in it overnight? Do you erase the centuries of brutality and ignorance and passion that preceded this enlightened era and left their mark upon the genes and characters?

When you teach that all is privilege, how do you enforce that privilege also implies responsibility? And for those who refuse to conform, how do you handle them?

Recently, on the air, someone said this: 'Young people are children callously pulling off the wings of butterflies. The chief purpose of education is to impart an understanding of the butterfly's point of view!'

The tragedy of our time is that we can fly jet airplanes, broadcast color television, make atomic power, but we're not sure how to bring up our children. And the record would indicate we're not doing a very good job of it.

Perhaps, we're spending so much time on the material advances we have forgotten children need attention too.!

Yet, all is not lost. We have many fine children today and out of the welter of things that are happening, we'll manage to struggle along and make it. Civilization always has, despite the dire predictions of the seers and the prophets.

Recently 4,000 student delegates to a high school convention in San Francisco adopted a set of 'teen-age Ten Commandments.'

They went like this: (1) Stop and think before you drink. (2) Don't let your parents down; they brought you up. (3) Be humble enough to obey. You will be giving orders yourself some day. (4) At the first moment, turn away from unclean thinking. (5) Don't show off when driving. If you want to race, go to Indianapolis. (6) Choose a date who would make a good mate. (7) Go to church faithfully. The Creator gave us the week, give Him back at least an hour. (8) Choose your companions carefully. You are what they are. (9) Avoid following the crowd. Be an engine, not a caboose. (10) Best of all—Keep the original Ten Commandments."

YOURS SINCERELY, JACK WILLIAMS!

End Notes

1. Edmund Spurr Whitman, *The History of the Phoenix Elementary School District No. 1. 1871-1983,* Ed. Sigrid Taillon Whitman, p.1.
2. ibid. p. 37.
3. Bradford Luckingham, *Phoenix/The History of a Southwestern Metropolis,* (Tucson: University of Arizona Press, 1989), pp. 147-8.
4. ibid. pp. 150, 179-180.
5. Ted Kazy, ©*The Arizona Republic**, November 6, 1955, p. 1.
6. ibid. p. 1.
7. ©*The Arizona Republic**, November 1, 1955, p. 6.
8. ©*The Arizona Republic**, November 4, 1955, p. 6.
9. Bill King, ©*The Arizona Republic**, April 18, 1956, p. 1.
10. ©*The Arizona Republic**, April 20, 1956, p. 6.
11. Bradford Luckingham, *Phoenix/The History of a Southwestern Metropolis* (Tucson: University of Arizona Press, 1989), p. 160-3.
12. Bernie Wynn, ©*The Arizona Republic**, November 9, 1966, p. 16.
13. Bernie Wynn, ©*The Arizona Republic**, November 1, 1966, p. 23.
14. ©*The Arizona Republic**, November 7, 1966, p. 27.
15. Bernie Wynn, ©*The Arizona Republic**, November 9, 1966, p. 16.
16. ibid. p. 16.
17. ©*The Arizona Republic**, November 5, 1970, p. 6.
18. Ronald B. Taylor, *Chavez and the Farm Workers,* (Boston: Beacon Press, ©1975), pp. 279-280. Used by permission
19. ibid. p. 280.
20. ibid. p. 280.
21. Athia Hardt, ©*The Arizona Republic**, May 31, 1972, p. A13.
22. Dr. John L. Myers, Ed. *The Arizona Governors 1912-1990,* Article by Dr. Nelda C. Garcia, pp. 133, 136.
23. ©*The Arizona Republic**, October 24, 1931, pp. 1-2.
24. Jana Bommersbach, *New Times,* April 25-May 1, 1990, pp. 28-9.
25. Jana Bommersbach, *New Times,* May 2-8, 1990, p. 18.
26. Orren Beaty, ©*The Arizona Republic**, November 30, 1952, p. 1.
27. Jana Bommersbach, *New Times,* May 2-8, 1990, p. 28.
28. J. Dwight Dobkins and Robert J. Hendricks, *Winnie Ruth Judd: The Trunk Murders,* (New York: Grossett & Dunlap, 1973), pp. 242-3.
29. ©*The Arizona Republic**, October 27, 1971, p. 1.
30. ©*The Phoenix Gazette**, October 12, 1968, p. 6.
31. Sam Lowe, *Scottsdale Progress,* November 8, 1969.
32. ©*The Arizona Republic**, January 31, 1970, p. 6.
33. ©*The Arizona Republic**, January 22, 1989, Obituaries, p. B11.
34. Arizona Board of Regents, *Minutes of a Meeting,* June 10, 1970, p. 3.
35. ©*The Arizona Republic**, January 22, 1989, Obituaries, p. B11.
36. Dr. Thomas Ford Hoult, *The March to the Right, A Case Study in Political Repression,* (Cambridge, MA: Schenkman Publishing Co., 1972), pp. 1, 3-5. Used by permission.

* Used with permission. Permission does not imply endorsement.

Index

Meet the Author

Frank Asbury was born in Phoenix, Arizona at St. Joseph's Hospital when it was located within a few blocks of Phoenix Union High School.

Most of his boyhood was spent in the Palmcroft neighborhood about a mile from Encanto Park. He and his cadre of friends spent so much time in the park they felt it had been created solely for their private enjoyment.

His most cherished youthful times were those spent on cattle ranch venues in Pleasant Valley, below the Mogollon Rim, and up on the Blue River southeast of Alpine. On the Blue were fashioned his memories of learning to ride horses, rope calves and assist in their branding, and of watching beavers build dams. He also learned about butter churns, taxidermy, farm tractors and "snipe" hunting.

His formal schooling began at Kenilworth Elementary and included passages at West Phoenix High School, the University of Southern California and Arizona State University. His education hasn't been completed yet!

Before entering radio broadcasting in Phoenix, other jobs included being a control tower operator in the U. S. Army, working for an ice company, working in produce sheds in Phoenix and Glendale and being a door-to-door milk man for Borden Dairy.

Asbury's broadcasting career began in Phoenix and included brief encounters with Houston, Texas and Albuquerque, New Mexico. Most of his radio work was done for KOY Radio in Phoenix where he was at various times, a disk jockey, talk-show host, sports director and news anchor. He also flew traffic watch airplanes for KOY. Following his tenure at KOY, he worked at KNIX Radio as a news anchor, then news director.

For his journalism work he has received awards from the Arizona Press Club, the Arizona AP Broadcasters Association, the American Bar Association and The Scripps Howard Foundation.

The author and his wife currently live in Chino Valley, Arizona.